RANDOM HOUSE

LARGE PRINT

THE TIME OF OUR LIVES

TOM BROKAW

THE TIME OF OUR LIVES

RANDOM HOUSE
LARGE PRINT

For Claire and Meredith,
Vivian and Charlotte,
and grandchildren everywhere

PREFACE

What happened to the America I thought I knew? Have we simply wandered off course, but only temporarily? Or have we allowed ourselves to be so divided that we're easy prey for hijackers who could steer us onto a path to a crash landing?

These were not questions I was asking in August 1962, when I was a newlywed and a rookie journalist. America was investing in a new generation of leadership and promise. John F. Kennedy was in the White House. Dr. Martin Luther King, Jr., was on the march in the South. Astronauts with the right stuff pointed their aspirations toward the heavens. Women were stepping out from behind their aprons and questioning their assigned roles. Young artists were giving new voice to music, film, and literature.

I couldn't wait to be a part of it all.

A half century later it is a much different world, and I am a weathered survivor of the rearranged American landscape, a familiar territory for me in my personal and professional life. Wherever I go I am asked, "What has happened to us? Have we lost our way?"

One often repeated question is the most troubling of all, because it challenges an American belief so fundamental it might as well be carved in stone on a Washington monument: "Will our children and grandchildren have better lives than us?"

Is that essential part of the American Dream disappearing? There are no simple, reassuring answers, and as a citizen, father, and grandfather, I am not immune to the worries that prompt the question. I believe it is time for an American conversation about legacy and destiny.

I am not a sociologist or a psychologist. I am a journalist, an observer, and a synthesizer—a man who has explored a lot of the world and been a witness to recent history. I have seen what enlightened leadership can accomplish, whether it is on a family, community, national, or world level. I've also been astonished by our capacity to make the same mistakes in one form or another again and again.

I have made my own share of mistakes, as we all have. They've yet to invent a GPS system for the best road to a secure and worthwhile future, but I do have some thoughts, original and inspired by others, for our journey into the heart of a new century. To begin, isn't it time to reflect on where we have been and how we are going to move forward together, and to do it with more listening and less shouting?

There is a good deal of debate these days about American exceptionalism—about who believes in it and who may have doubts. I have no doubts. But I also believe that the unique character of America is very much like my definition of patriotism: Love your country but always believe it can be improved.

That was the unspoken way I was raised by a family of patriots and mentors who represented a broad spectrum of political and cultural notions but shared a common belief in the American Dream and a determination to constantly renew America's promise. Those indelible lessons from family and friends are still with me, and I hope you will find them familiar and worth renewing as they play out across the chapters that follow.

What I know for sure is that many feel America is adrift, and the time to build the future is now. We will be judged not simply by the cacophony of those on the left and right with access to a cable system or a blog but rather by the tangible legacy we leave behind.

This immigrant nation—this destination for those looking for economic opportunity, political freedom, and the realization of dreams—has confronted great trials in the past and prevailed. We can draw on those experiences and find new ways to address the challenges that await us now.

As I learned in the first decade of this new century, there are daring new ideas being tested in the laboratories of everyday life by bold and unconventional thinkers and doers. You'll hear their voices and learn their ideas in the pages that follow.

Academics tell us that centuries and decades are imperfect ways to measure the long curve of history. Perhaps, but for me every decade of my life, beginning with the forties, had a bold punctuation mark, so I had more than a little curiosity about what a new century might mean to us. The defining events of the first sixty years of my life were about to recede. What should we all expect next?

What follows are the observations, hopes, memories, and suggestions of a child of the twentieth century who had big dreams fulfilled beyond his boyhood fantasies. I am now a man of the twenty-first century, with some observations on how we might realize the great promise of a future that would benefit us all.

It was a New Year's Eve unlike any other in my lifetime, and possibly yours.

On December 31, 1999, I stood on the top-floor terrace of the Renaissance Hotel, high above Times

Square in New York City, looking down on the revelers jammed onto every square millimeter of sidewalk, curb, gutter, and street—an estimated two million who were giddily anticipating the beginning of a new century and a new millennium. We were part of a vast global gathering witnessing the turn of the clock from the momentous events of the twentieth century—what had been called the American century—to the unknown events of a new calendar. There was a rolling wave of euphoria about the moment and apprehension about the unknown as the clock struck midnight around the world.

I was fifty-nine years old, a long way from my heartland roots, immersed in journalism, successful in my marriage and professional life, and a relatively new grandfather. I had reported on most of the major events of the previous four decades, from the triumphs, tragedies, and turmoil of the sixties in America through the resignation of a U.S. president, the collapse of the Soviet Union, the emergence of China as a political and economic force, wars in the Middle East and Central America, the birth of twenty-four-hour cable news, the still-evolving and transformative effect of cyberspace, and, at the time, a cheerful celebration of prosperity in ever more layers of American life.

While I tried to offer our audience some perspective on what this new, twenty-first century might bring, it was, in retrospect, a modest effort.

My friend and competitor Peter Jennings was across the way, anchoring an impressive and much more ambitious ABC News production on the turn of the century, as he demonstrated one of the marvels of our new age: communication by satellite and via Internet, which allowed him to instantly call up colleagues in China, Australia, Africa, and elsewhere, and bring the global party to his glassy studio in midtown Manhattan.

The airwaves that night were filled with commentators in every language on every medium, grasping for the phrase that might put two thousand years in perspective and prepare their audience for the next two thousand.

The biggest concern at the time was Y2K, shorthand for the year 2000. Would all the computers that formed the central nervous system of the world's financial markets, transportation systems, and communication networks—and were vital to commerce, medicine, law enforcement, and even entertainment—recognize the changeover from years beginning with "19" to "20"?

They did, and the dancing in the streets continued uninterrupted.

A few exceptionally prescient flags were raised. Writing in **The New York Times**, Louis Uchitelle warned about the likely possibility of a big down-turn in an economy so dependent on a booming stock market. He cited the "wealth effect," when a rising market encourages consumers to spend more and borrow more. "A market sell-off," he wrote, "would throw the effect into reverse. The spenders would pull way back. Companies would, too, in response. Job growth would halt; the unemployment rate would rise and incomes would fall. But debt would not."

Eight years later that warning became reality as the sharpest, longest downturn in the American economy since the Great Depression knocked over our house of cards and spread around the world. It was nothing less than a Great Recession, a deeply painful time and a cautionary tale, the lessons of which should be attached to every birth certificate and all new citizenship papers for the next century.

That 1999 **New York Times** analysis laid out with commonsense clarity the inherent structural weaknesses of America's spending and debt binge. It was one of the few exceptions to the otherwise conventional wisdom dispensed during the millennium festivities. But on such an occasion, who noticed?

I admit that I didn't. Nor could I fully grasp the personal effect of moving past middle age and becoming a grandparent. My wife, Meredith, is now known as Nan, and I am Grandpa Tom, or sometimes just Tom. Beyond the nomenclature, grandparenthood brought with it wonders and worries about the world my descendants will inherit. Will their future be defined more by constraints than by expansion? No one that New Year's Eve foresaw the attacks of 9/11 on America or their monumental consequences, including the two longest wars in our history.

What to make of all this? Of the time gone by, of the America that my parents' generation and my generation knew, and of America's present and future—its promise for our children and grandchildren? My ideas about the times my family lived through and the lessons we can take from them were still unformed that night, when the chime of history's clock signaled that the twenty-first century had begun.

Another kind of clock is a fixture in our family and in my memory of a time gone by. It's a grandfather clock with a simple yet elegant face of black Roman numerals against a white background framed by polished fluted brass. The pendulum, a highly polished brass orb the size of a serving platter, is connected to the clockwork by nine alternating brass and lead rods, and it swings with a slow-dance grace.

The clock was a prominent feature in the lobby of the weathered wooden frame hotel founded by my great-grandfather in Bristol, South Dakota. The Brokaw House, as it was called, catered to the workers and passengers of the booming railroads chugging across the grasslands.

The clock is part of my earliest memories of family and place. It has made its way through four generations of the Brokaw family, from the Dakota Territory to California, Washington, D.C., and New York City. The clock now presides over the rustic dining room in our century-old ranch house on the edge of the Montana wilderness. When my mother visits we always remark on how it has been more than a timepiece. It is, in its own way, a witness to our lives and to all the changes we have experienced.

Almost every family has a piece of furniture or photograph or favorite place that represents a connection between the past, the present, and the future. We count on them to bind us together, and we cling to them as familiar icons when the future begins to challenge the past.

With my mother at my side I looked at the family clock with a fresh appreciation of all we'd been through and how far we'd come, and I tried to imagine what a new day will bring. When Mother returned to California after her last visit, I looked up at that fixed sight in the farmhouse and thought

The Brokaw timepiece.
It has been in our family for a hundred years.

about our family, about other families, and about America, past, present, future—the time of our lives in the twentieth century and into the twenty-first.

The clock has been such a constant that I'd taken it for granted as just another decorative piece in our living quarters, until that moment. Perhaps because of my own acute awareness of time left, of having our grandchildren visit here with their parents and my mother—four generations under one roof—I watched the magisterial sweep of the second hand and the minute-by-minute, hour-by-hour passage registered on its stately face with a new appreciation of all that it has witnessed: generations past and present of the Brokaw family, and by extension, the American family.

The clock has a soft tick tock, tick tock that has measured so much change, large and small.

Tick, tock. The arrival of electricity and telephones to the remote reaches of rural America, places still untamed no more than 120 years ago.

Tick, tock. Steel mills and railroads, automobiles and airplanes, oil fields and amber waves of grain, new cities and new industries beginning to fulfill the promise of the twentieth century as the time America came of age.

Tick, tock. World War I, the Roaring Twenties, the soaring stock market and its sickening crash, the Great Depression and a landscape of despair.

Tick, tock. The rise of Adolf Hitler and his maniacal followers, the spreading stain across Mother Russia where a revolution in the name of workers' rights gave way to brutal oppression on a historic scale.

Tick, tock. Pearl Harbor and the end of American innocence about its fortress invulnerability. World War II, fought on six of the seven continents, in the skies above and the seas below. More than fifty million people perish. The world is introduced to a new form of madness, the Holocaust. The beginning of the nuclear age and the Cold War between one colossus in the east and another in the west.

Tick, tock. An unparalleled prosperity sweeps across America, giving rise to a middle class that anchors an economy of home ownership, good wages, college education, and the expectation that every generation will enjoy more than the last.

Tick, tock. The race to space in the heavens and the chaos of generational upheaval on the planet below. Vietnam opens wounds still not entirely healed. America confronts the shameful realties of two societies, one black, one white, separate and unequal. A president brings the country to the brink of a constitutional crisis before he is forced to resign.

Tick, tock. The dissolution of the Soviet empire,

the rise of a new China, and the enterprise of Pan-Asia. Islamic rage and more wars. Personal computers, the Internet, and a wired and wireless world. Medical miracles and environmental anxieties. An African American president is elected, and a severe economic recession shatters confidence in long-held assumptions on the fundamentals of American security.

The family clock keeps on ticking, requiring from time to time a winding up or some delicate maintenance. Our children and grandchildren pass by, glancing at its hands to measure the time of an appointment or the hours left in the long daylight of Montana summer days. In their digital world it must seem to be a curiosity or a useful relic, but perhaps one day they, too, will use it as a calibrator of great, wrenching change.

As a journalist and a fully engaged citizen, I am both excited and more than a little unnerved by the magnitude of the changes we have seen and the prospect of those yet to come. We are swept up in a cosmic storm of new technologies that are at once unifying, liberating, and terrifying. We are living through "the Second Big Bang": A new universe is being formed in cyberspace and we're trying to determine which of these new "planets" will support life and which are merely distractions; which will drift too close to the sun and burn up and which will flourish. Will we master this astonishing technology or become hostage to it?

These are not unique questions. Every new technology frontier generates concerns about wise use and societal impact. Steamships and flight; automobiles, electricity, and telephones; antibiotics and X-rays; nuclear power and space travel: All prompted speculation about benefits and penalties.

But nothing has changed the world as swiftly or as dramatically as the power of cyber technology and its capability of retrieving, sharing, and acting on information about everything from a good cup of coffee to the best treatment for a rare form of cancer, from buying a multibillion-dollar corporation to starting a revolution.

How, then, should we use this technology to create a national dialogue on what we want for our grandchildren—mine, Claire, Meredith, Vivian, and Charlotte, or yours—and those who may be yet to come? How will those future generations think of us? What personal values and public citizenship commitments will we leave them? How will we respond, now and going forward, to the manifest challenges facing all of us in the brief time we have on this precious planet?

Long after I am gone, with some gentle care, the Brokaw clock should still be in the family, its rhythmic cadence measuring the passage of new generations and reminding them of what has gone before.

What do we have to offer those who will be examining our time and accomplishments?

To begin, a suggestion to remind us of our most fundamental obligation: It is time to reenlist as citizens.

Tick, tock.

CONTENTS

PART ONE

Getting the Fundamentals Right

CHAPTER 1

Generations

FACT: In every century of America's history we have been the beneficiaries of sacrifice and selflessness in the face of great odds to build a stronger country: The Founding Fathers of the eighteenth century fought a bloody revolution for freedom. The great losses of the Civil War were necessary to preserve the union. The pioneers who pushed west endured countless hardships as they opened the rest of the continent. The generation that came of age in the Great Depression helped save the world in World War II and gave us modern America.

QUESTION: A hundred years from now, what will be our indelible and measureable legacy? What will our grandchildren say of us? Of our country? Historians will not judge our time by Barack Obama, George W. Bush, or the Tea Party alone. We're all in the dock.

This book really began when I found myself at the intersection of history and my life while on assignment in Europe. It was June 5, 2009, a cloudy day with intermittent rain showers, and I was standing on the terrace of the Royal Palace in Dresden, Germany, awaiting the arrival of the young president of the United States, Barack Obama, for a **Today** show and **Nightly News** interview.

Mentally, I reviewed the loose ends of my appointment: What should I ask about his upcoming visit to the notorious Nazi concentration camp Buchenwald? How would he compare his challenges as president with those of Franklin Delano Roosevelt during the Great Depression and World War II? What did he plan for his speech the next morning, at the sixty-fifth anniversary of the Normandy invasion?

In several personal trips to that stretch of Norman beach and the windblown headlands, on solitary walks through the simple white headstones at Colleville-sur-Mer, the American cemetery where so many young Americans are buried, I have come to see the invasion as what should have been a template for our modern world. It represented political cooperation and vision; military genius; and courage, sacrifice, and shared determination to defeat a great unambiguous evil. It was a distillation of all the heroic efforts to roll back the darkness of fascism and make the world, if not perfect, then more just.

Now I was with a young American president who would face his own tests of vision, courage, and political acumen in the twenty-first century. For the moment my more prosaic considerations were dictated by the imperatives of broadcast news. Was the **Today** show ready to take in the video feed, edit the interview, and get it in shape for that morning's telecast? Given the subject and the setting, these are the occasions when great thoughts should prevail, but they would have to be deferred until the logistics were satisfied.

President Obama arrived right on schedule, surrounded by his posse of top aides. He strolled with his easy athletic gait along the walkway of the magnificent Baroque building, past the priceless porcelain vases collected by Saxony kings, and gave me a soft shout-out. "Hey, Brokaw—we're here."

THE PAST

This was in the early months of his first term and he was casually confident, as yet untested and, oh, so young. He had just arrived from Cairo, where he had given a well-received speech to the Islamic world on the need to find a more peaceful path to the future. I had just come from Berlin, where, I told him, I had been the night the wall came down in 1989. He laughed and said, "I remember; I watched. I was in law school at the time."

What?

Law school? And you're now the president? I was about to be fifty when the Soviet Union collapsed; it was just yesterday in my life, and he was at Harvard, a student with a promising but unresolved future.

After a moment or two of casual banter the president took his place and with his characteristic ease responded to questions about the Holocaust, Iranian president Mahmoud Ahmadinejad, Israel, his great-uncle's experience in World War II, and the moral character of the American people.

That character, he suggested, has to be refreshed. "The biggest lesson we learned from World War II," he said, "is America can do anything when it puts its mind to it, but we gotta exercise those muscles."

He went on, "I think they've atrophied a bit. We're soft in ways that are profoundly dangerous to our long-term prosperity and security." Here he hesitated slightly. "And, you know, we—we've gotta start working those—moral muscles and service muscles and sacrifice muscles a little more. That's still in the American character, and I'm confident we'll be seeing it in the years to come."

As he was leaving, I suggested he try to find a solitary moment the next day when he would be in Colleville-sur-Mer, the American cemetery on a bluff above Omaha Beach. "Walk through those headstones with just your thoughts," I said, "and be prepared to have your knees buckle."

As I have learned in more than a half-dozen visits to that landscape of simple white tombstones, the initial response of first-time visitors to the American cemetery, and the beaches, is often tearful, but I was confident such a walk would generate more than an emotional reaction for the president.

The lingering lesson of Omaha Beach is the deeply affecting value of common cause supported by uncommon valor against monstrous tyranny. It is a lesson that need not be reserved for great wars alone.

Since my first visits to Normandy, Pearl Harbor, and other World War II battle sites, I've often been unduly agitated by petty feuds or tempted to abandon vexing problems that require more personal investment than I anticipated. Then I imagine being strafed in a surprise attack or wading off a Higgins boat into the face of withering fire and knowing that if I survive it is just the beginning of another year of hellish combat, lost buddies, and horrific sights. It is a useful perspective and, judging from the personal accounts of strangers who have approached me over the years to describe their visits to Normandy, it is a common reaction.

In Dresden, the cloudy skies brightened and I took my place for the **Today** show transmission, which went smoothly.

I've been in this line of work for almost half a century and while a presidential interview is always memorable, the following day you're off to another development, in pursuit of another news maker, asking, "What's next?"

This time, however, the occasion, setting, circumstances, and subjects lingered. I wondered how this young president and all of us would be tested anew. The answers came swiftly enough, especially for President Obama. Following a triumphant tour, the president returned home to the realities of a severely broken American economy—one so shattered it had ignited a national dialogue about values and proportion, greed and appropriate reward, and the role of the government in the marketplace.

Unemployment rose from 8.1 percent in March 2009 to a persistent 9.6 percent in the summer and fall of 2010 and then to 9.8 just before the midterm elections. That number didn't reflect those off the statistical grid who had given up looking for work. Confidence in the young president and his team drawn largely from the academic and political worlds plummeted heading into November.

President Obama was vilified as a socialist out to destroy the country, and questions were raised about his birthplace, despite a newspaper account and evidence from the state of Hawaii that, in fact, he was born in that state on August 4, 1961.

A national libertarian movement called the Tea Party arose out of a rage against government spending, anxiety about the economy, and the perceived distance between the priorities of Washington and those of grassroots America.

The president's failure to aggressively attack unemployment and his concentration instead on a massive and complex health care reform law troubled even his most ardent supporters. By the fall, national polls showed that by a margin of four to one, likely voters felt their personal finances were worse off in the last few years.

The president and his team responded by relying on the power of personality, sending Obama into the heartland for backyard sessions with "just folks" and into large rallies with the party faithful.

Meanwhile, the Tea Party derided a federal stimulus program, reform of the big financial institutions, and an auto industry rescue as more examples of government run amok. In fits and starts Obama tried to find his voice as a populist and then as a healer, but the troubled economy resisted his charms and policies.

Nothing worked.

In the November 2010 congressional elections, the president, in his own word, took a "shellacking." Democrats lost sixty-three seats in the House, dropping to their lowest level in that chamber since 1940. They barely hung onto the Senate, encouraging Republican Mitch McConnell of Kentucky to immediately announce his goal was to deny President Obama a second term.

THE PRESENT

More unexpected dramatic and consequential change was just over the horizon in a part of the world where America remained deeply involved in the longest wars in its history—in Iraq and Afghanistan, and by extension Pakistan.

The president, the CIA, and the U.S. military gave the world a startling and welcome May Day 2011 surprise. They ordered a nighttime raid deep into Pakistan to attack a fortified compound in a bucolic residential area where they suspected Osama bin Laden was living.

The president made the call to proceed with the high-risk mission. A Navy SEAL team helicoptered across Pakistan from Afghanistan on a Sunday to make the strike, and it was brilliantly executed. Osama bin Laden, the number one terrorist in the world, was killed in the raid. No Americans were wounded or lost.

President Obama's credibility as a leader, a cool and courageous commander in chief, soared briefly just at a time when the country was expressing deep doubts about those qualities for his management of the economy and his reaction to earlier, unexpected developments in the Middle East.

The administration and most of the world had been caught off guard by events that profoundly reordered the political and physical landscape of the region. When a Tunisian fruit vendor committed suicide by setting himself on fire to protest his homeland's autocratic and corrupt government, news of his desperate act spread across the Islamic world, including Egypt, the most populous of the Middle Eastern countries and a close ally of the United States.

Demonstrators took over Cairo's central city, demanding the resignation of President Hosni Mubarak, who had ruthlessly ruled his country for more than thirty years, mocking Egypt's constitutional guarantees of free elections.

In the opening days of the uprising, the Obama administration steered an uncertain course, publicly calling for its ally Mubarak to leave immediately and privately pleading with him to institute a succession plan that would play out over several months.

Finally, Mubarak, pushed by his own military, stepped down. Demands for democracy and more economic opportunity spread throughout the region. It was the beginning of a new era in the world's most volatile region and a dramatic reminder to the United States that its reliance on Middle Eastern oil and nondemocratic regimes was long overdue for a reset.

The seething of the underclass spread to Libya, where Moammar Gadhafi responded with vicious military attacks on the insurgents that drew international condemnation and resulted in NATO military help for the Libyan rebels.

Saudi Arabia's rulers, the most important economic allies of the United States in the Middle East, ordered military action against protestors in their country and sent troops to help Bahrain suppress an uprising there.

As this populist rebellion played out across Yemen, Syria, and more moderately in Jordan and Saudi Arabia, I went to the region to take the measure of the uprising's depth and long-term effects in a region where we have such a high-stakes investment in oil, counterterrorism, and the need for political and military stability.

From the souks of Iraq to the presidential palaces of Jordan and Saudi Arabia there was a consensus on only one conclusion: The Middle East would never be the same. Just how it would be altered and what the consequences would be, no one could say. An Iraqi street merchant said to me, "Democracy is good but look at us. It is so hard."

Abdullah II, the forty-nine-year-old energetic, American-educated Hashemite king of Jordan, told me, "This time will define my monarchy; I will spend every day for however long it takes to expand political participation in our country. We need to have a representative government."

In Saudi Arabia, the ruling family was much more guarded. Prince Saud Al-Faisal, the seventy-year-old foreign minister, acknowledged the government must be prepared to make some changes but, alluding to the United States, he emphatically added, "A Middle Eastern country has to change itself; if you have interference from the outside it can only be detrimental."

Not surprisingly, the prince also blamed the tensions in the Middle East on Israel for failing to find a way to accept the establishment of a freestanding Palestinian state.

The so-called Arab Spring was another reminder that the Middle East's lethal mix of zealous tribes, faiths, ambitions, autocrats, and arsenals is a hair trigger for violence. It pumps more oil and gas than any other region in the world and its interfaith rivalries are like something out of the Middle Ages. Israel is a heavily fortified presence in a sea of antipathy.

In March 2011, global chaos spread to Japan in the form of a monstrous earthquake that triggered a tsunami so destructive it will surely be the stuff of legends for centuries to come. The tidal wave was followed in quick order by a catastrophic breakdown of Japanese nuclear facilities, the ultimate modern-age nightmare.

Japan was gravely wounded by these calamities and the long-term recovery prospects did little to help the American economy, given the strong trade relationship between the two countries.

The failure to have sufficient safety standards in place at their nuclear plants, the chaotic and unsuccessful attempts to head off a meltdown, and the terror of long-term radiation poisoning are colossal failures for a culture that not so long ago was widely praised as the future of the world.

With the Middle East uprisings and the Japanese calamity, President Obama learned again, as all presidents do, that it is the unanticipated and unexpected events that can be the most perilous for a chief executive. He had already been buffeted by the great BP oil blowout of 2010 in the Gulf of

Mexico—an environmental disaster, a management crisis, and a severe strain for the "no drama" Obama style.

Other modern presidents have faced unexpected assaults on their carefully ordered promises of expanded peace, prosperity, and renewed pride in all things American.

John F. Kennedy, who pledged to "fight any foe" in the "long, twilight struggle" against Communism, nearly stranded his presidency on the shoals of the Bay of Pigs and then successfully finessed what could have been a nuclear Armageddon in the Cuban missile crisis.

His successor after the fateful Friday in Dallas, Lyndon Baines Johnson, started on a high note of national unity, a breakthrough on civil rights, and a landslide election win, only to spiral down into forced retirement as a result of his anguished but stubborn prosecution of the Vietnam War. His final year in office was marked by assassinations, racial rage, and mounting war losses, culminating in the election of his archnemesis Richard M. Nixon, thwarting all that Johnson had hoped to accomplish.

Nixon brilliantly opened the way to China and reorganized the federal government into a much more efficient model, but he remained hostage to his Cold War instincts in Vietnam. At home, the deep, dark side of Tricky Dick led to an imperial presidency of vendettas against so-called enemies and disregard for the rule of law. His Oval Office was a bunker stocked with illegal conspiracies and presidential high crimes and misdemeanors.

We survived all of that and the subsequent stumbles of succeeding presidents. Gerald Ford, the healer, didn't prepare the nation for his pardon of Richard Nixon. We gave Jimmy Carter his chance and then moved on to the sunny optimism of Ronald Reagan, who recast the role of the federal government, got entangled in Iran-Contra, and so skillfully kept the pressure on the Soviet Union that its end was inevitable. George H. W. Bush impressively managed the fall of Communism and a war against Iraq but failed to deal with a short, sharp recession in the last year of his term.

Bill Clinton, the first boomer president, brought youthful energy and a different Democratic Party to the White House, lighting up the skies with a bright, bright economy before succumbing to his worst personal failings and standing trial in an impeachment. George W. Bush and the rest of us were blindsided by 9/11, the terrorist act that led to the two longest wars in our history and to continuing questions about Bush's judgment in foreign policy and in his stewardship of the economy, which went into free fall during his final year in office.

That Polaroid portrait of our recent history is offered as a reminder that our strengths and prominence, our size and influence, bring with them commensurate assaults on our well-being. We have the world's most robust democracy, most powerful economy, most dominant military power, and most ambitious values agenda, but we are not impervious to the riptides of envy and competition.

THE PROMISE

The drumbeat of problems for President Obama and, by extension, for all of us did not end with the 2010 midterm election.

The Great Recession and all of its political and economic consequences; the rise of China and India; the upheaval in the Middle East; the wars in Iraq and Afghanistan; the massively destructive earthquake, tsunami, and nuclear meltdown in Japan; the environmental calamity of the Gulf of Mexico oil spill; the economic disarray in the European Union; the lawlessness throughout Mexico, our southern neighbor—all represent a confluence of problems that, taken together, are unparalleled in the American experience in the post–World War II era.

We've experienced grave crises before but never so many all at once representing such a wide range of disastrous possibilities: the new world DIS-order.

Add to that the polarization in the political and governmental institutions in Washington, D.C., and we have a historic set of challenges that demand attention and action that go well beyond a testy exchange on cable television or a food fight in the blogosphere.

Those atrophied muscles of the national character that the president mentioned in Dresden demand our attention. Can they be developed so that they provide the strength to carry us through this treacherous passage? Do we have the will to restore a sense of national purpose that unites us rather than divides us? Shouldn't we take a realistic inventory of our strengths, needs, objectives, and challenges as we head into a new century in a changed world?

None of us has all the answers, but so many of the problems are self-evident that we should begin by first addressing those that threaten our core vaues: political pluralism, broad-based economic opportunity, national security secured by means other than the barrel of a gun, cultural and religious tolerance.

The first step: Establish a climate for listening as well as for shouting.

What better time than now, when we've been through the searing, frightening experience of a historic economic setback? What better time than now, when our principal political, economic, and cultural competitors are expanding at a breathtaking pace, especially in educating their young for the demands of a new age.

As time goes by, we'll have fewer ideal opportunities to reignite the American Dream and face the territory ahead with a renewed sense of who we are, where we've been, and where we're determined to go.

The lessons of just the past decade are self-evident. The big picture for American primary and secondary education was a canvas of discordant colors and composition. Republicans and Democrats alike were enablers in the wave of easy credit, big government spending on the pet projects of congressional power players, and the launch of two wars simultaneously with no realistic means of financing them beyond the much-too-optimistic scenarios for success.

The plethora of historic challenges before us didn't start with the inauguration of President Obama, and those challenges will not end with the next election cycle, whoever is the victor.

We have miles to go before we sleep, as Robert Frost reminded us.

We can learn from the past as we grapple with the present and work to renew and fulfill America's promise.

CHAPTER 2

One Nation, Indivisible

FACT: It's now accepted that independent voters make up about 30 percent of the American electorate, and with every new election they're proving to be a powerful swing vote. In 2008, President Obama won in large part because he had an 8 percent margin among independent voters; by the midterm elections of 2010, independents favored Republicans by 18 percent.

QUESTION: When was the last time you voted a straight party line?

That great American philosopher P. J. O'Rourke, a former hippie, now a New Hampshire country squire, sums up the self-righteous nature of the two major American political parties well when he says, "Democrats are the party that says government will make you smarter, taller, richer and remove crabgrass from your lawn. The Republicans are the party that says government doesn't work and then they get elected and prove it."

O'Rourke has also observed that "America wasn't founded so we could all be better; America was founded so we could all be anything we damn well pleased."

THE PRESENT

In a nation of so many voices, all of them, it seems, with access to some kind of megaphone, whether it's call-in radio talk shows, Internet blogs, or rallies on the National Mall or in a town square, the American political character is to some degree in flux. In a 2010 Gallup poll to determine the ideological makeup of the country, people identifying themselves as liberals were outnumbered by those who call themselves conservatives by a two-to-one margin, but moderates were within five percentage points of the conservative bloc.

The 2010 numbers were a big gain for conservatives, who trailed moderates in the last term of President George W. Bush. The percentage of Americans identifying themselves as conservative was the highest in Gallup's polling history. Much of that, no doubt, was a result of the stratospheric levels of federal debt piled up, beginning with the Bush years and accelerating in the first half of the Obama term, twinned with the persistently high levels of unemployment and the anxiety over the new national health care plan.

The upswing in the conservative numbers paid off for the Republican Party in the midterm elections, obviously, and GOP leaders once again began speeches with the phrase "The American people have spoken." Just two years earlier, Democratic Party leaders were using the same phrase, and four years before that President Bush was invoking the American people in his speeches.

Six months after the Gallup poll, an NBC survey found that 79 percent of the respondents thought the country was too divided politically. That's a very big number, but it didn't surprise me, because everywhere I go, whatever the ideological or cultural makeup of the audience, that is the overwhelming sentiment of the audience when the talk turns to politics.

For me there was no more poignant demonstration of the frustration over the cold war among partisans in Washington than an encounter I had on Capitol Hill. Two bright young men approached me after a reception for the International Rescue Committee, a renowned refugee organization with bipartisan support. They were dressed in the standard uniform of Capitol Hill aides: serious blue suits, white button-down shirts, and red ties. One said, "Mr. Brokaw, we want to ask you about the old days here in Washington." Given their youth, I was afraid by "the old days" they meant the first Clinton term, but I volunteered to help however I could.

They went on, as one gestured to the other, "We're best friends even though he's a Democrat and I'm a Republican. We go into Georgetown, drink beer, and argue politics and at the end of the night we're still friends.

"But his boss is a Democratic congressman and mine is a Republican and they won't talk to each other. It's really frustrating. Was it always this way?"

I explained that no, it wasn't. When I worked in Washington at the height of the Watergate scandal, an acrimonious time, Meredith and I would often find ourselves at dinner parties with prominent Republicans and Democrats, sharing a drink and stories from some dustup on the Hill. Senators Bob Dole and George McGovern, I told them, two World War II veterans representing opposite ends of the political spectrum, are close friends and often worked with each other on fighting global hunger.

If anything, the partisan cold war in Washington has gotten worse since that chance encounter with members of a younger generation determined to serve but frustrated by the consequences of the fundamental incivility that courses through Washington these days.

My friend Bob Schieffer, host of the highly regarded Sunday morning public affairs program **Face the Nation,** has been in Washington more than forty years and he says it's never been worse. He cites a prime example of the juvenile behavior that takes place on too many Sunday mornings when he tells of one show in which he had one Republican guest and one Democratic.

The Sunday shows all have what is called a "green room," where the guests and journalists gather for coffee, makeup, and any last-minute instructions. Bob told me, incredulously, "We had a call from the staff of one of the men, a senior leader of the Senate, requesting separate rooms so the guests wouldn't have to be together. I said, 'No. We're not changing our behavior just to suit theirs.' "

House Speaker John Boehner was asked on NBC's **Meet the Press** to review a video of some Iowa citizens who believe President Obama is a Muslim and that that guides his policies. Moderator David Gregory asked the Speaker if he felt compelled to correct those voters. Boehner declined, saying his job is "not to tell the American people what to think."

The Speaker said he believes the president when

he says he is a Christian and that he accepts the state of Hawaii's declaration that Obama was born there, making him an American citizen, but he chose not to say that those who believe otherwise are wrong. As I watched, I wondered what the Speaker would say if a panel of voters told a moderator that Mitt Romney, a Mormon, is a member not of a real Christian faith but rather a cult, or that Ron Paul is a fascist. Would the Speaker not strongly challenge those erroneous beliefs?

When confronted with similar allegations early in the 2008 campaign, Senator John McCain, running for the Republican presidential nomination, quickly corrected an Obama detractor. McCain said, "Obama is a decent person and a person you don't have to be scared of to have as president."

Slashing rhetoric and outrageous characterizations have long been part of the American national political dialogue—Abraham Lincoln was portrayed as a subhuman ape in the highly partisan newspapers of his time—but modern means of communication are now so pervasive and penetrating they might as well be part of the air we breathe, and therefore they require tempered remarks from all sides. Otherwise, that air just becomes more and more toxic until it is suffocating.

Personally, I'd like the partisan combatants on both sides of the aisle to explain their attitudes to a junior high civics class. Maybe their adolescent audience could teach them some manners and lessons in teamwork.

These days anyone who enters the public arena is immediately cut from the herd and ear-tagged like a critter on a cattle ranch. Cable television anchors, radio talk-show hosts, and blogosphere commentators tag anyone who crosses their line of sight, and once on, the tag is tough to remove.

On Fox News, the scarlet-letter tag is "liberal," attached with a sneer. Keith Olbermann has special enmity for conservatives, for a while tagging a number of them as "the worst person in the world" during his popular run as an MSNBC commentator.

I've found myself in both camps, especially in election years.

In the closing days of the 2008 election I was attacked from the left when, on an episode of **Meet the Press** with guest John McCain, I reminded our viewers that it was the anniversary of his capture in Hanoi during the Vietnam War. Earlier in that campaign, the liberal blogosphere lit up when I reported on **Meet the Press** that the one area in which Barack Obama continued to trail McCain was the public's confidence in his qualifications to be commander in chief.

To my mind, those were two relevant, objective facts worth noting in a campaign, but to the ideologues on the left, they certified me as a conservative sympathizer. The right is even more vigilant for any perceived signs of liberalism, picking over every utterance, written phrase, or personal reflection.

For a public person this comes with the territory, but sometimes the reach is exaggerated to the point of being amusing. On occasion, when asked about the place of racial issues in the campaigns, I've said that my perspective is helped by the personal realization that in the early, formative stages of my career I was aware that if my skin pigment had been one shade darker I would have been denied opportunities at every turn, in Omaha, Atlanta, and Los Angeles.

Rush Limbaugh took to the airwaves to declare me a "self-hating liberal." Rush, of all people, should know that those of us who make a very good living listening to the sound of our own voices are incapable of self-hate. We think we're grand, and I include Rush in that fraternity.

Rush is at least an original, and his power is indisputable. He relishes his influence and the financial rewards that come with it. However you regard his message or personal style, he has earned his fortune by creating an enormous audience of the faithful, or "ditto-heads," as they like to be called.

A ditto-head is someone who worships at the altar of Limbaugh's preaching, never questioning his conclusions or reasoning. Equivalents can be found on the left as well, slavishly loyal to the shibboleths spouted by the liberal faithful. You'll find very little self-doubt or second thoughts on left-leaning websites such as Daily Kos or MoveOn.Org.

THE PAST

More than twenty years ago, a wise American who had served at the highest levels of the academic, public, and corporate world warned against just such a condition in American life.

He was John Gardner, a PhD graduate of Stanford University; U.S. Marine Corps officer during World War II; president of the Carnegie Foundation for the Advancement of Teaching; secretary of health, education, and welfare in the LBJ administration (he quietly resigned over Vietnam); and board member of the Shell Oil Company, American Airlines, and Time, Inc., among others.

Gardner founded Common Cause, the citizen-based organization that brought together disparate groups to work on the problems of a changing America. He was also a member of President Reagan's task force on private sector initiatives.

Few members of America's leadership class had the depth and breadth of his experiences, and fewer still commanded the personal and professional respect that Dr. Gardner did. He embodied what the Founding Fathers must have had in mind when they envisioned a republic of engaged citizens.

As Gardner watched the rise of special interest groups across the political and economic spectrum in the sixties, he had serious concerns. In his seminal book **On Leadership,** Gardner wrote, "Unfortunately a high proportion of leaders in all segments of our society today . . . are rewarded for a single-minded pursuit of the interests of their group. They are rewarded for doing battle, not compromising."

In a chapter called "Fragmentation of the Common Good," he asked,

How many times have we seen a major city struggling with devastating problems while every possible solution is blocked by one or another powerful commercial or political or union interest?

We are moving toward a society so intricately organized that the working of the whole system may be halted if one part stops functioning.

He continued, "A society in which pluralism is not undergirded by some shared values and held together by some measure of public trust simply cannot survive." That was written more than twenty-five years ago and is truer now than it was then.

To emphasize his point, Gardner concluded, **"Pluralism that reflects no commitment whatever to the common good is pluralism gone berserk."** The italics were his, to underscore his concern.

I miss John Gardner as a fellow citizen. I came to know him personally, and I was always impressed by his quiet but forceful commitment to the common good. We have too few of those voices these days.

THE PROMISE

Another was the late A. Bartlett Giamatti, Renaissance literature scholar and president of Yale University. I collected his speeches, including the one he made to the incoming Yale freshman class in 1980. He said to these bright and no doubt anxious eighteen-year-olds that he understood their unease. "What is the point of it all?" he guessed they might be wondering. "And will anyone tell me or am I expected to know?"

Giamatti, a true Renaissance man in his scholarship and wide-ranging interests, then reminded the class of something I trust they carried with them through Yale and beyond. "You are not expected to know," he said, "but you are expected to wish to know."

What better advice for a young man or woman on the cusp of what passes for the real world? Think. Reason. Explore. Question.

He went on to raise a rhetorical question—"Why does any ideology tend to be authoritarian?"—and then answered it: "These closed systems are attractive because they are simple and they are simple because they are such masterly evasions of contradictory, gray, complex reality. Those who manipulate such systems are compelling because they are never in doubt."

To a later class of Yale, he noted that the twentieth century was coming to a close. "The fact is," Giamatti said, "nothing is old or tired or declining for you. You are new. You do not need the worn intellectual cloaks of others; you must weave your own, with which to walk out into the world." He sent them on their way with a charge to be remembered by all: "Do not become one of those who only has the courage of other people's convictions."

Dr. Giamatti left Yale for his other passion: He became the commissioner of Major League Baseball, a game he loved and wrote about with the pen of a poet and the hard lessons of a lifelong Boston Red Sox fan.

"Baseball," as he so memorably put it, "breaks your heart."

It is designed to break your heart. The game begins in the spring when everything else begins again, and it blossoms in the summer, filling the afternoons and evenings, and as soon as the chill rains come, it stops and leaves you to face the fall all alone. You count on it, rely on it, buffer the passage of time. To keep the memory of sunshine and high skies alive, and then, just when the days are all twilight, when you need it most, it stops.

I became acquainted with Giamatti while teaching a guest lecturer course on politics in the television age in the late seventies. He monitored my course and invited me to lunch after I wrote a whimsical piece in **The New York Times** about grade inflation at Yale. I had lamented the absence of grade inflation during my undistinguished undergraduate years at the University of South Dakota, and apparently some of the Yale faculty were not amused.

Bart was on my side, laughing as he encouraged me to keep assigning term papers and grading them on a meritocratic scale.

When he died at age fifty-one in 1989, America lost a brilliant scholar and a brave, wise voice.

Gardner and Giamatti's counsel to find a way into the future **together** without absolutely surrendering our most cherished beliefs takes on a new urgency when we contemplate these numbers: There are a little more than 311 million of us now. By 2050, that number is expected to exceed 440 million. That means more efficiency and cooperation will be required in every part of our lives, from jobs to food, politics to security, medicine to energy, culture to education.

We have much to learn, and the schoolhouse is a place to begin.

CHAPTER 3

K Through Twelve and the Hazards Along the Way

FACT: The U.S. Department of Education estimated in 2010 that more than forty million Americans are functionally illiterate. According to the federal agency, 10 percent of students at four-year colleges take remedial reading courses. American fourth and eighth graders rank, respectively, eleventh and eighth in the world in international science aptitude tests. By grade twelve, American students are near the bottom of the international scale. America's African American and Hispanic minorities are much further down the scale in reading, math, and science.

QUESTION: In 2010, President Obama's big educational initiative, Race to the Top, offered states a total of $4.35 billion in grants to change their education policies to make them more effective. That is less than what the Department of Defense spent in Iraq in June of the same year. Does that make sense to you?

In 1983, the National Commission on Excellence in Education issued a report called **A Nation at Risk: The Imperative for Education Reform**. It concluded that the foundation of the American education system was being eroded by a rising tide of mediocrity that threatened our future as a nation and as a people.

That report was issued almost two decades ago, before China and India began moving up the economic food chain. By 2009, the United States was falling even farther behind. American fifteen-year-olds ranked twenty-fifth out of thirty-four countries in math, fourteenth in reading, and seventeenth in science.

What does that tell you about their ability to meet the even greater demands of higher education or to be prepared for the modern workplace?

The American Dream is freighted with so many interpretations it defies a tidy, all-inclusive definition, but if there is a common denominator it is education. It is part of our country's promise and lore, from Abe Lincoln educating himself by the light of a fireplace, to the kind of rural one-room schoolhouse my mother attended, to the power of our vast system of higher education, stretching from the ivied halls to the new for-profit institutions and all the large and small public and private colleges in between.

Five years after the **Nation at Risk** report, I was in Seoul, South Korea, for the Olympic Games, which were being telecast by NBC Sports. NBC News had a significant presence because there were reports of possible terrorist attacks taking place during the games. It was showcase time for Korea, which had begun to flex its well-toned industrial muscles in the world markets.

Because of the time difference I anchored **Nightly News** at 5:30 A.M. Seoul time. We broadcast from a building roof overlooking a local junior high school. The first morning when I finished at 6:00, I was startled to see the school courtyard crowded with uniformed students, hunched over their textbooks, studying by flashlight, waiting for the doors to open at 6:30.

They were there every morning during my stay. I returned to America to share that story with friends and audiences. I would be met with smiles of appreciation, but through the nineties American education remained stuck in old conventions and failing schools.

I was reminded of that Seoul experience when I read U.S. education secretary Arne Duncan's account of a meeting between President Obama and South Korean president Lee Myung-bak. Duncan recalled President Obama's asking his Korean counterpart, "What is the biggest challenge you have in education?"

President Lee answered, "The biggest challenge I have in education is that the parents are too demanding."

THE PAST

Those South Korean parents share a cold, rocky peninsula with a lunatic nuclear-armed regime just to the north. China hovers over them like a dark storm cloud, ominous and intensely competitive. China tried to conquer South Korea in the early 1950s, and when the United States rushed to its aid in the first shooting war between the West and China, nearly thirty-four thousand Americans died.

At the time of the war, South Korea was, by twentieth-century standards, a primitive, agrarian society; a large portion of the population lived as they had a hundred years earlier. The national literacy rate was not much above the nineteenth-century standard, and the industrial economy was only a faint promise of what was to come.

Thirty years later, South Korea had become an industrial and electronic colossus, the fifth largest producer of automobiles in the world. Samsung,

Daewoo, and Hyundai were filling American stores with state-of-the-art electronic appliances. Per capita income in South Korea went from nine hundred dollars in 1952 to twenty-eight thousand by the early part of the twenty-first century, much greater than in Brazil, Russia, India, or China, the foursome known as BRIC for their muscular economic potential.

South Korea's meteoric rise in industrial productivity and prosperity did not, of course, go unnoticed.

I once interviewed a Russian member of the young intellectuals Mikhail Gorbachev promoted in a futile effort to save Communism in the Soviet empire. When I asked him just when it was that he realized the Russian system was failing, he said, "When the South Koreans came to Moscow with all of their prosperity; their automobile business and electronics. They did that in such a short time and here we were, a much larger nation with so many more resources, still so far behind."

Now, as we rocket our way through the twenty-first century, South Korean parents are still demanding more education, better schools, higher standards. South Korean school years are 220 days long, and it's estimated that South Korean parents spend up to 30 percent of their income on education, including hiring tutors, for their children.

They have millions of counterparts in China—

where the economic expansion has been even more dramatic—and in India, Vietnam, and Singapore. To resort to a sports metaphor, those are the teams the U.S. children will be playing against in the twenty-first century. Do American parents have it within themselves to demand as much from the classroom as they do from the Little League coach or Saturday soccer officials?

Ask almost any American parent what they'd like for their children and the answer is likely to include "a college education," even if the child in question is a skateboard slacker who's spent more time at juvenile hall than in a classroom. However unrealistic the chances are for some individual students, twenty-first-century America as a whole needs a higher college graduation rate and more emphasis on math and sciences if we're to compete in the international arena, where our chief rivals are pouring money, resources, and students into educational systems designed to meet the needs of a modern, technological world.

Reorganizing American education is a priority on a level with containing the war on terrorism, for it is just as essential to national and economic security.

As it now stands, education in America is an uneven landscape, shaped by income and community priorities. In every measurable way, it is the economically poor—including white students but mostly racial minorities—who have been left behind by political indifference, apathy within their culture and communities, or a combination of both. With the competitive demands of the twenty-first-century global economy we can ill afford to be a nation deeply divided by the skills, education, and access to economic stability these fundamentals foster.

Reforming public education is to the twenty-first century what the civil rights movement was to the mid-twentieth century. It is nothing less than a national imperative to maintain the health of our country's status.

Education is a massive problem, but as developments along several fronts have demonstrated, it is not insoluble. Unconventional and impressive efforts at the local, state, and national levels have broken the chains of low expectations and stereotypes. Many of these efforts represent what I believe will be an important movement for America in the twenty-first century: public-private partnerships to address the systematic dysfunction eroding the undergirding of American society, from education to health to public service and beyond.

In an effort to describe for myself and others the place of education in society I've settled on the familiar phrase "the coin of the realm," for a well-educated population is the strongest currency to take to the international marketplace and to advance the place of a pluralistic society on the home front.

Now, at least, the urgency of educational reform has been acknowledged.

As the debate over public versus charter schools heats up school board meetings, op-ed pages, and think tanks, my own experience leads me to believe that a mix of public and private is the best approach. Plainly there are areas where public school parents need another choice for their children. However, successful public schools and the role they play as anchors in neighborhoods and communities ought not be discarded.

The expanding public-private model is part of a growing nationwide trend to involve other parts of the public sector as well as private enterprise in the essential task of education. These new efforts are deeper and more systematic than the old model of a service club or private benefactor offering a medal or a modest scholarship to the top students in each graduating class.

In every state there are encouraging examples.

THE PRESENT

In Mississippi my friend Jim Barksdale took a big chunk of the fortune he made as CEO of Netscape, the breakthrough Internet browser, and set up a foundation with the ambitious goal of eliminating illiteracy in his home state. Mississippi consistently ranked at the bottom of the public education performance scale. Barksdale and his late wife, Sally, donated $100 million to a program run by Jim's brother out of the University of Mississippi to improve teaching techniques in the state. When the Barksdales decided on literacy as their cause an estimated seven hundred thousand adult Mississippians were reading below the eighth-grade level.

The Barksdale Reading Institute (BRI) sponsors in-depth research on improving the way reading and writing are taught, and works to increase parental involvement with students, emphasizing early childhood development. BRI contracted with four Mississippi school districts to place its own principals on the job with authority to develop curricula, hire teachers, set grade expectations, and organize schedules.

"We believe the ability to read and education are the core to anyone's life, economic and social," says Jim. He had firsthand experience with reading difficulties as a third grader. His parents could afford a tutor and he caught up with his peers, but he's often wondered what would have happened to him if he had not gotten the extra attention.

The Barksdale Reading Institute is one of several

corporate and private efforts around the country to improve education performance and opportunities at the local level.

None is more impressive than what a philanthropic Georgian developer launched in a run-down Atlanta neighborhood that was home to an equally run-down golf course, East Lake, where the legendary Bobby Jones played his first and last rounds of golf. In the post–World War II years, East Lake began a slide into a dark pit of drugs, violent crime, and shattered families. It was such an urban war zone it became known as Little Vietnam.

Local police estimated the local drug trade was a thirty-five-million-dollar-a-year business; the crime rate was eighteen times the national average. Almost two-thirds of the residents were on some form of welfare, and fewer than one-third of the students graduated from high school.

Enter Tom Cousins, a wildly successful developer of many of Atlanta's most prestigious structures. Cousins, an aw-shucks Georgia native and golf enthusiast, had a bold idea: Restore East Lake Golf Club and use it as an anchor to revitalize the neighborhood. With like-minded friends, he established the East Lake Foundation to do just that.

Cousins said he got the idea when he "read that in New York seventy percent of the inmates in the state's prison system came from just eight neighborhoods." When Cousins inquired about the Georgia inmate population, he got a similar answer. He decided to do something about that in the East Lake neighborhood.

When he approached the president of the University of Georgia, his alma mater, the president immediately told him it was a bad idea. Cousins replied, "I've wasted a lot of money on other people's bad ideas. Now I'm going to waste some on one of mine."

Cousins knew from experience that it was not enough to simply build new low-income housing. He wanted to change the whole environment, from housing to schools, from opportunity to role models. "A child has no control over where he or she is born," he told newspaper columnist Leonard Pitts. For the children in East Lake, "the future was set and hopeless." Cousins was honest enough to admit he doesn't know what would have happened to him if he'd been raised in that environment.

So with the proceeds from the restored golf club, the East Lake Foundation built a community of mixed-income housing at affordable prices so stable families would be attracted to the area. The shabby public school was razed and replaced with an ultramodern charter school named for Charles R. Drew, a pioneering African American physician who was instrumental in developing blood plasma

Tom Cousins with students from his
East Lake project

processing and storage. Dr. Drew died in 1950 but, given the success of the school that bears his name, he lives on in ways he could not have imagined during his lifetime.

Before Cousins and his friends got involved in East Lake, just 5 percent of local fifth graders were equal to their contemporaries in state math levels. In 2010, ninety Drew students were selected to participate in the statewide MathFest, a tribute to Drew's ranking as the number one school in Georgia for math scores.

More than 90 percent of Drew students met or exceeded the state standard in math, language arts, and reading in 2010, and a Drew student won the Atlanta Public School System spelling bee.

When my colleagues at CNBC produced a documentary on Cousins and his East Lake project, his friend Warren Buffett saw it, called Cousins, and asked, "How can I help?" One of the founding fathers of the hedge fund industry, Julian Robertson, wanted in as well.

So the three of them established a new foundation called Purpose Built Communities to replicate the East Lake model in other cities, including the washed-out neighborhoods of New Orleans.

Buffett, who sizes up people as he does the companies in which he makes an investment, says flatly of Tom Cousins, "I'd invest in anything he does;

he's one of my heroes. He's just a very good guy—smart, modest, and with great values."

Tom worried that maybe failure was a fixed part of the culture of low-income minorities but, he told me, "All they needed was a chance. We just helped them get that opportunity." Tom Cousins and his wife, Ann, are proud of what they've created in East Lake, but what impressed me when we talked about it was their determination to keep the success focused on the families and children who are turning their lives around.

Up north, in Cincinnati, the East Lake equivalent was Taft High School, an inner-city school failing on every level. The graduation rate in 2001 was 21 percent. The state declared Taft an academic emergency with fewer than half the students proficient in reading and just 25 percent proficient in math.

That year the Cincinnati Public School District decided to try a bold approach. It renamed it the Taft Information Technology High School and sent in principal Anthony Smith to turn it around.

Smith made some quick fixes, such as ending the two-hour lunch period and shaping up the tutoring program. He went door-to-door in the neighborhood and asked the families for help in transforming the school, explaining that his "covenant was with the community, not necessarily with the board of education." Local residents knew the penalty of not having a good education. Half lived below the poverty line, and just over half had a high school diploma.

Smith kept the old staff and teachers, meeting with them to determine what was working and what wasn't. He also appealed to their pride by asking, "How does it make you feel to be possibly the worst school in the state of Ohio?" During a faculty conference he told the teachers that if they weren't prepared to sign on to his program they shouldn't return after lunch. They all came back, ready to try a new approach.

But for all his energy and inspiration, Smith couldn't do it on his own. Fortunately, he met Jack Cassidy, the hard-driving CEO of Cincinnati Bell. Cassidy is a leading member of Cincinnati's impressive business community, which also includes Proctor and Gamble, a major General Electric division, Kroger, and American Financial Group.

Cassidy was stunned by what he learned about Taft. "My God," he said, "as a taxpayer and a citizen, can we really have this as a place we call a center of education?" Cassidy soon coined a new motto for Taft students: "Go big or go home."

The transformation of the school and its mission soon drew students from areas outside the neighborhood; they were attracted by more than the name. Cincinnati Bell underwrote a new computer lab, and Bell employees volunteered as tutors.

The company also offered a cellphone and a computer to any student who maintained a 3.0 grade point average, and installed high-speed Internet broadband in neighborhood homes, because, as Cassidy explained, "College exists on the Internet."

When I asked Cassidy why he got involved, he said it was a mix of civic and corporate duty. "Why shouldn't America's inner cities be capable of the same kind of growth? Besides, as a capitalist, I want a return on my investment. Business is the consumer of the product that schools produce, and academics have lost a sense of that.

"We did it because we believed it would create better customers and better employees. World economic growth is coming from countries that not long ago were thought of as 'Third World economies.' Look at China.

"But," he cautioned, "business should not control the curriculum. There is a danger in letting business write the history books. And it's not just about dollars. Trillions have been spent on education. We don't need more money. We need better content that produces results."

Cassidy goes to Taft football games and other school activities. He also gives out his personal cellphone number so students can reach him directly. "It keeps me engaged," he says, "and it tells the kids

Jack Cassidy, CEO of Cincinnati Bell,
and Tony Smith, principal of Taft High

they have no excuses unless they've exhausted all the opportunities, including talking to me."

Success doesn't start and stop with one school in Georgia or Ohio. Business and educational leaders have reached out to other innovators, such as the former New York City schools chancellor Joel Klein, to get fresh ideas.

In New York City, Mayor Michael Bloomberg has made education reform and improvement a centerpiece of his administration. The system was shaken up first internally by Chancellor Klein. He took on the teachers' unions, fired principals, and encouraged the development of more charter schools and magnet public schools. When some charter schools failed to live up to the new, higher standards, he closed them down.

He also had help from New Visions for Public Schools, a collection of nonprofits and community organizations that partnered with new schools on a wide range of issues. The New Visions website provides access to papers on all the relevant issues of modern education, from teacher training to techniques for improving attendance. As for a credo, New Visions says partnerships mean all stakeholders are responsible for the city's youth.

As part of their stakeholder mission, Chancellor

Klein and other community and philanthropic groups pressed the New York state legislature to lift the cap on charter schools within a school district. Old-line New York politicians, many of them closely aligned with the teachers' unions, resisted but were forced to accede to the community's wishes.

When Klein retired, Mayor Bloomberg stumbled in naming his replacement. He chose a friend, magazine publishing executive Cathleen Black, who was enthusiastic but woefully unprepared for running a massive, complex public education system with well-entrenched and outspoken constituencies. After just a few months on the job, she stepped down at Bloomberg's request, and he named Deputy Mayor Dennis Walcott as her replacement.

Walcott comes from the streets of the borough of Queens, a man who has always worked within the system whether as a teacher, social worker, head of the New York chapter of the Urban League, or deputy mayor. If he succeeds, he can affirm what a lot of veteran educators are saying: Schools can be reformed from the inside as well as from the outside.

Amanda Blatter knows that. The success of the charter schools and the support they received did not escape the attention of the more enterprising public school teachers and administrators. Blatter, the energetic principal of PS 109, an elementary school in the South Bronx, went to many of the same benefactors of the charter schools and said, in effect, "Hey, I need help, too."

She outlined plans to convert a barren second-floor book-free space back into the library it once had been and added a new twist: make it a community study center for residents of the surrounding impoverished Hispanic neighborhood and invite parents to use it in the early evening as a study hall with their children.

Blatter was so successful that she raised enough money for a full complement of computers and e-readers. On the day she dedicated the facility, the students poured into the room and powered up the computers and e-books, accessing their favorites beneath a banner that read "A room without books is like a life without a soul," the observation of Marcus Tullius Cicero.

A few weeks after the dedication, Blatter told me, "The library has been an amazing success. Children are visiting every day and checking out so many books we need to significantly increase our inventory. We have the library open two nights a week until six o'clock for parents taking English as a second language—ESL—classes."

Amanda Blatter and her faculty worked hard before the library was rebuilt to make PS 109 one of the best-performing schools in the South Bronx.

They now feel they have an opportunity to do the same for the neighborhood and the parents.

Blatter is a reminder that with all the attention focused on charter schools and the role of outside interests, dedicated and gifted public school teachers and administrators continue to show up every day. They are more than instructors and managers, there only to collect a paycheck and benefits. They're surrogate parents, community advocates, and a vital link between hope and despair for their charges.

At Jack Britt High School in Fayetteville, North Carolina, students have a similarly creative principal, Denise Garison. She attacked student and community indifference with a bold, unconventional approach. She was frustrated by the constant gap between the test scores of white students and those of her African American and Hispanic students. Whites consistently scored almost 13 percentage points higher. She refused to accept the whispered stereotype that the minority students just weren't as bright.

So she dug into the records of the underperforming students and found that many of them were chronically absent and came from families where school failure was endemic—passed along from generation to generation.

Garison went to her teachers and challenged them to change the game at Jack Britt High, just as a new coach would challenge his staff and the community to improve the record of a losing football team.

Teachers responded by spending more individual time with the at-risk students identified in the survey; they even handed out their own email addresses so students could be in touch when they encountered homework problems. In a radical departure from convention, Garison persuaded the school district to pay twenty dollars an hour to teachers who volunteered to be at the school on Saturdays from 8 A.M. to 4 P.M. so students could get extra tutoring on standardized tests. When that money ran out, many of the teachers voluntarily showed up on Saturdays without compensation. A community organization provided the Saturday school lunch.

Jack Britt student Teshiya McClean was failing everything as a freshman, but when her teachers began to take a special interest in her, she responded. By her senior year she was on the school honor roll. "I am very proud," she says. "They taught me I can do anything I put my mind to."

This aggressive approach at Britt has paid off. The gap between white students and their African American and Latino counterparts has narrowed to under 5 percent.

In the end, it comes down to what Jack Cassidy

Denise Garison at Jack Britt High School

in Cincinnati calls "the moral responsibility of all of us to leave the country and its institutions better than what we found."

In Cincinnati that moral responsibility is embodied in a school that is going from worst to first. Taft's graduation rate in ten years went from 21 percent to more than 95 percent. Proficiency in math and reading jumped to 95 percent in the same period.

PS 109, Jack Britt High, East Lake, and Taft are striking examples of what author and businessman Wes Moore calls "environment versus expectations." Moore, an African American, was raised in minority neighborhoods in Baltimore by a single mother after his father died when he was three. He was a bright but indifferent student, more interested in scoring points in playground basketball games than on classroom tests.

When he was in the eighth grade his mother arranged to send him to a military school. He rebelled against the discipline and tried repeatedly to run away in the first month, but his mother kept sending him back.

Slowly he learned something about himself. "I liked being a leader," he told me. "I was responsible for my squadron and that gave me pride." That pride began to show up in the classroom and soon he began making his mark in academics as well as on the parade ground, basketball court, and football field.

Moore came up against another reality. "I learned it's a much larger world than my old Baltimore neighborhood," he told me with a laugh. "I thought I was pretty hot in basketball, that I could dunk on anyone, but I quickly learned there were others who could dunk on me."

It never occurred to Moore than he might be a candidate for a Baltimore school he barely knew about: Johns Hopkins University, one of the elite academic institutions in the world. "No one in my old neighborhood thought about going to Johns Hopkins," he said. "We all thought we were going to the NBA."

Moore's military school record was so impressive he made it to Johns Hopkins, and there the new expectations for his life carried him even higher. He became the school's first African American Rhodes scholar, then an officer in the elite U.S. Army Rangers and served in Afghanistan. He returned to the United States and became a White House fellow, working alongside Secretary of State Condoleezza Rice in the State Department.

All this he documented in detail in his **New York Times** bestselling book **The Other Wes Moore,** a model for understanding and addressing the issues of education and expectation in the inner cities of America. It is the story of two young men, both named Wes Moore, raised a few blocks from each other, each by a single mother. One's life was defined by the temptations and perils of the drug trade, a violent, lucrative, and lawless society in almost every big-city minority neighborhood.

The errant young man tried once to get loose of the hold drugs had on him by applying to Job Corps, but he failed and returned to a life of crime. He was eventually involved in a robbery in which an off-duty policeman was killed. The "other Wes Moore" went to prison, and when the author's mother told him of the coincidence of their names and childhoods, a lesson began to take shape.

The Rhodes scholar Wes Moore asked to see the felon Wes Moore in prison, and a visit was arranged. They met more than a dozen times, exploring why one had found such a rewarding life while the other ended up in a penitentiary. When Moore asked the inmate if he thought the environment in which he grew up was the cause of his fate, the answer was, "No, it was expectations. No one expected anything of me," adding that when he began to develop a police record, his troubles multiplied. He dropped out of school and moved deeper into the underworld of his community.

During one of their conversations the prisoner Moore said to his new friend, "Listen, I have wasted every opportunity I ever had and I am going to die in here so if you can make a difference, you should do it."

That prompted Moore to write the book about two men, same name, different fates, and to use their starkly different lives as a call to service in education. He says, "Teachers, tutors, mentors, and volunteers who work with young people are as important to our survival and advancement as a nation as the armed forces."

Moore carries that message with him everywhere, and this unique story combined with his passion and charismatic personality has landed him spots on national television shows and a featured role at the 2008 Democratic National Convention. He works with returning veterans from Afghanistan and Iraq to ensure they have the educational opportunities they need to advance their lives, and he does the same for Baltimore kids caught in the criminal justice system.

While doing this, Moore has a full-time job in financial services but, as he says, "Public service doesn't have to be an occupation but it must be a way of life." For boomers and other grandparents, public service as a school volunteer should be a natural calling—an extension of their formative years when they set out to change the world.

THE PROMISE

Boomer or other grandparent volunteers can meet and work with a new generation of like-minded activists such as Geoffrey Canada, who runs the Harlem Children's Zone, an educational and community services oasis in the heart of Manhattan's storied African American neighborhood.

The Children's Zone grew out of the desperate need to do something about the destructive effects of the crack cocaine epidemic of the eighties, and it has proved to be a model of public and private cooperation, providing everything from parenting workshops to classes on how to control asthma, a persistent health threat in the area.

Canada presides over more than one hundred city blocks of programs and services designed to offer hope to local families, with the emphasis on education and preparing youngsters to take their place in a society beyond their 'hoods. He runs a tight ship, constantly monitoring the effectiveness of programs within the Zone. Those that don't measure up lose their funding, and he moves the money to those that get the job done.

Michele Rhee, the dynamic and iconoclastic former chancellor of the Washington, D.C., school system, embodies what a very modern school administrator can become.

Rhee, a striking and hard-driving Korean American single mom, had no experience as even a junior high principal before she was hired to fix one of the most broken systems in the country. She was a teacher in Baltimore who had attracted attention for her work in Teach for America.

She came to the nation's capital and immediately began to raise hell with a school district that was a collection of parental and teacher union fiefdoms, with a student population in constant turmoil. Rhee began by firing hundreds of principals and teachers and replacing them with principals and teachers with proven track records. She took on parents' groups and consolidated schools to get the efficiencies she needed.

Perhaps Rhee's most controversial innovation was a program called "Capital Gains," in which students received money for good grades and good behavior. They could earn as much as two hundred dollars a month. She worked out an arrangement with a local bank for the students to establish accounts so they could develop money management skills.

When I visited Rhee at Shaw, one of her middle schools in northeast Washington, she laughed as she recounted critics saying, "You're paying kids to come to school? Since when do you gotta pay kids to come to school?" Rhee responded, "The crazy thing is not that we're paying kids to come to school. The crazy thing is that for decades we allowed kids **not** to come to school and didn't do anything about it."

Rhee had no illusions that handing out money for good grades and behavior is a silver bullet solution. As she put it, "Not one thing will turn the district around; it's going to be fifty different strategies and initiatives that add up to success."

While visiting Rhee, I got an insight into how "Capital Gains" had very practical implications. One of the programs involved assigning students roles—for example, a married mom with two kids, a single man, and so on. The students were then given a checkbook with a phantom balance in it and told to do the family's shopping for food, clothing, and other necessities.

One student told me, "I wasn't that good at math so I thought it was a good project, but I knew it would be hard to do. We had to pay bills, look for houses, go to the store. Get groceries. We're learning how to deal with real life."

I teasingly said, "If you could fix the economy, that would be a big relief to all of us."

A member of the class immediately shot back, "We're working on that now."

Michelle Rhee and Brian Betts,
the enterprising principal she recruited
from the Maryland suburbs

In an economy that is growing more and more complicated, with difficult decisions to be made about health care policies, choosing a pension plan, finding or refinancing a mortgage at favorable rates, sizing up bond or mutual funds, preparing a tax return, and calculating currency exchange rates, fundamental instruction in consumer finance should be as much a part of every school's curriculum as basic math and English. We can hope this early training will temper young people's attitudes toward thrift and credit card debt, and give them pause when a mortgage broker slides a subprime loan across the desk and says, "Hey, I can get you into a big home for no money down and interest only for ten years."

Rhee's aggressive approach was just three years old, and the results in student performance were encouraging, but time ran out before her systems could be fully realized. Her patron, Mayor Adrian Fenty, was defeated in the Democratic mayoral primary after one term for what was widely believed to be his aloof manner, especially with fellow African Americans in the poorest neighborhoods. Shortly thereafter, Rhee resigned.

In a joint statement to the city that is such a curious combination of wealthy and poor blacks, old-line white neighborhoods and the citadels of government and corporate power, Fenty and Rhee acknowledged that when it came to ensuring broad support for their efforts, they fell short.

Nonetheless, they were justifiably proud of the progress district students had made in a little more than three years. They urged the entire community to get behind the new mayor in his efforts to continue the progress. "We have laid the foundation," they said, "but the hardest steps are yet to come."

In the short time she was in the job, Rhee came to believe fervently that the old claims about ethnicity and zip codes as an excuse for failing grades are more about the general failing of society than about children and their families. She also recognized that schools must value the students.

The embodiment of that sentiment was the principal at Shaw Middle School, Brian Betts, a cheerful, athletic white Southerner who made a name for himself as an administrator in the wealthy, leafy suburbs of Montgomery County, Maryland, next door to Washington and light-years away in terms of income, family stability, and expectations for students.

Within a few days on his new job, Betts, who had a phenomenal memory, was a fixture on the schoolhouse steps every morning, in rain, sleet, or snow, greeting his hundreds of charges by name and cheering them on for the day ahead.

Dana, a student who had been suspended ten times a year earlier, became a model student. Why?

"Mr. Betts. He's a very positive person and he has a good attitude. And being around people like that lifts your spirit. It helps you be a better person. So it's all about Mr. Betts."

It was not just a parlor trick for Betts. He told every student that he cared about them.

Tragically, Betts was murdered in his home in the spring of 2010. Two young men he met online were charged with killing him and stealing his car. His death was front-page news in the nation's capital, and his students and their families mourned deeply for weeks, with good reason. Not enough inner-city students have a Mr. Betts experience.

The absence of a teacher who is also a surrogate parent is not a condition confined to African American or Latino children. In the 1980s, in a documentary called **To Be a Teacher,** I interviewed Lenny Stanziano, who taught math in Toms River, New Jersey. He, too, stood at the schoolhouse door and greeted students by name, saying he was often the first person to acknowledge them that day.

Many of his students were white, working- and middle-class kids, who lived with single parents or in households where both parents rushed off to work before dawn. Every student I talked to had high praise for Mr. Stanziano as a teacher and because he saw them as someone other than just a name in roll call.

Stanziano worked weekends in a large liquor

store, stacking beer cases in the refrigerator to supplement his meager teacher's salary, which was just over twenty-six thousand dollars in 1976. His classroom skills and commitment to education paid off. For the past eleven years he's been principal of Toms River High School South.

Can we take a moment to remember Mr. Betts? And hope for more Denise Garisons and Lenny Stanzianos?

They're out there in small and large school systems across the country. I've come across them in Los Angeles, Milwaukee, Omaha, Montana, rural Texas, Georgia, and Maine—the foot soldiers of American education: dedicated and inspirational teachers and administrators who for six to eight hours every day take responsibility for educating, comforting, and protecting our nation's most precious resource, its children. It is hard and noble work and, yes, it is not always done perfectly, but the failures of the system ought not to be blamed on the teachers alone. We all have a stake.

CHAPTER 4

Old School Ties and New World Requirements

FACT: The best economic argument about education is in the numbers, period. With every passing year more education means more income in the short and long term. The median annual income for a wage earner with a bachelor of arts degree is $55,700.

On average, that's close to $22,000 more annually than a high school graduate can expect to earn. Wage earners who have completed just some college courses earn on average 17 percent more than high school graduates.

QUESTION: What exactly does higher education mean in a modern global society, and how should it be organized for the masses as well as for the intellectually and financially elite?

For all the income advantages of a college education, there are mitigating numbers as well. The increasing cost of higher education is a number that has to be factored into the dividend of getting a degree. College graduates entering the workaday world in the middle of an economic downturn may not do as well as, say, a high school graduate with a capacity for fixing or demystifying a computer program.

The societal value of a well-educated citizenry is self-evident, but no one should have any illusions about the demands of the global economy. When young people with obvious aptitude announce they're going to college to be a "mass com" (mass communications) major, adding that they hope to be an anchor on a news program shortly after graduation, I have to temper my reaction.

While I try not to discourage them, I explain that the best journalists I know studied political science, history, economics, or biology, adding that they mastered their professional craft by working the police beat or covering the school board, city hall, or state legislature.

"Taking any economics courses?" I'll ask. "Or accounting or computer science or biology? How about writing?" The eagerness of my new young friends often turns to unease. "What is he talking about?" they seem to be thinking. "I want to be Diane Sawyer or Matt Lauer, not some wonk."

I was equally frustrated when a bright young African American student who won state honors at a Mississippi high school science fair announced he would be a marketing major when he enrolled at Boston University. He stuck to his plans despite my gentle efforts at dissuasion, and he graduated with honors in marketing. I am sure he'll be a success. It's his life, after all, but does America need another marketing executive rather than another scientist?

THE PAST

In the nineteenth century, a little remembered Vermont politician inspired a federal program that became one of the most important and enduring contributions to the development of modern America. It was the establishment of land grant colleges, the inspiration of Justin Smith Morrill, a Vermont congressman and later senator, who correctly surmised that the young nation needed a network of institutions to promote agricultural education, the mechanical arts, and military tactics, three pillars of nineteenth-century America. Now there is at least one land grant school in every state.

The needs of our society have, of course, changed over time.

A half century ago, when I was preparing to leave for college, I'm not sure anyone in our family even knew what that meant, exactly. Neither one of my parents had attended college, nor had any immediate relatives. Our high school had no organized college counseling program. In my graduating class, maybe half planned to attend college.

The University of Iowa was my only choice, and as an out-of-state student my total costs for the year were around two thousand dollars, including room, board, books, maybe a beer or two (okay—maybe more), and a modest but presentable wardrobe. Mother and Dad had saved for this big moment, and they sent me off with all their working-class hopes to be realized. I had a good public school education in the social and physical sciences.

I had saved a couple of hundred dollars on my own for the first year and enrolled in general liberal arts courses, thinking maybe I'd go to law school at some point.

Meredith's parents were both college graduates and so there was some family tradition, but this was 1958 and young women were not often encouraged to prepare for demanding careers, nor did their parents have the same expectations for them as they did for the young men of our time. Two of our brightest high school friends, both male, were recruited by Harvard with generous financial assistance. Meredith and three or four other young women should have been candidates for Wellesley or Smith or one of the other so-called Seven Sisters, but as she remembers, it never came up.

To the astonishment of her daughters today, Meredith made her entire college wardrobe at her Singer sewing machine. She was a skilled seamstress, and frugality was encouraged in her family. In her first year she attended a small women's junior college in Missouri. When she was crowned Miss South Dakota in 1959, she qualified for a scholarship to an in-state school, so she transferred to the University of South Dakota.

As Meredith puts it, her dad thought she'd go to college and get a "Mrs." degree.

Fortunately for me, that worked out, but I've often thought about how unfair it was that she and several other young women didn't have a crack at an elite institution. For most of us at that time, I suppose, the goal was to get an education, get married—often right after graduation—then get an advanced degree or a job and start a family. This was 1962, and the future seemed to be an exciting challenge for our generation, with a new, young president, John F. Kennedy, summoning us to rise to the occasion.

Russia was the major international concern, and many of my friends plunged into engineering classes as the nation's industrial infrastructure geared up to meet the Sputnik challenge, when the Soviets beat us into space. In my political science classes I read about missile throw weight and the larger question of how to conduct foreign policy in the nuclear age, in a seminal book by a little-known Harvard professor by the name of Henry Kissinger.

China was Red China, a closed, mysterious, and primitive cult with hundreds of millions of people marching in lockstep to the incantations of Chairman Mao. On the map of the world China might as well have been one of those blank spaces on the cartography of ancient mariners that read "Beyond here serpents lie."

Japan was beginning to produce a little car called Toyota and inexpensive electronics.

Korea was still struggling to recover from the bitter and costly war that had so deeply divided that forbidding landscape. The United States was sending military advisers to a place called Vietnam, which the French had abandoned not too many years before.

The overwhelming majority of students in American institutions of higher learning were white and from public schools. Most, I would guess, were adequately prepared academically for what was expected of them. The graduate schools—law, business, medicine—were dominated by white males. However misrepresentative that student profile may have been of the general population, it was adequate to the needs of a country that was so dominant in the world economy.

THE PRESENT

First-rate educations are available at what were originally land grant colleges—and not just at the best known of them, such as the University of California–Berkeley, Cornell, or Michigan State; they're available at the smaller state institutions as well. South Dakota State University is the archrival of the school where I finished my undergraduate studies, the University of South Dakota, but I have to give State, as we call it, full credit for turning out important scientists, business leaders, political leaders, and educators.

However, in the Great Plains states, as the population grows older and the young move on, taxpayers' priorities change, and money spent on higher education struggles to maintain its place in the state budget.

The charge for future generations in rural America is to make those schools even more competitive in a global environment, and to do that, the more sparsely populated states will have to make tough decisions. In the early part of the twentieth century it was politically and practically popular to have a number of taxpayer-supported colleges scattered throughout the state, because the agricultural economy meant farm kids had to divide their lives between class and harvest time. Now it is a drain on resources to have so many schools in various locations—resources that should be more efficiently applied to fewer campuses.

Wouldn't the state budgets and the population be better served by consolidating administrative costs and higher education resources on a regional rather than state-by-state basis?

The cost of higher education, the elixir of a progressive society, is rising at an alarming rate. According to the College Board, published tuition and fees at public four-year colleges rose almost 5 percent a year beyond general inflation from the 1999–2000 school year to the term that started in 2009. Private college tuition and fee costs went up a little more than 2.5 percent above inflation during the same period, but private schools started at a much higher level.

A working- or middle-class family hoping to send a child to a public four-year college—an institution paid for with their taxes—must, on average, pony up between eight and twelve thousand dollars just to get through the gate. That does not include computers, books, travel, wardrobe, laundry, social activities, or myriad other costs of just living.

So if an insurance broker, school principal, or factory manager is making ninety thousand dollars a year and hopes to send his or her two kids to the local state college, more than 20 percent of the family's gross annual salary disappears the day they're accepted.

The College Board, which oversees higher education testing and monitors college trends, conducted a study showing that a full 10 percent of 2007–08 college graduates had borrowed forty thousand dollars or more. That's more than two hundred thousand college graduates with more than forty thousand dollars in debt as they start careers and, perhaps, families. How does that affect their ability to buy a home, finance more education, or raise a child?

These debts were accumulated just as the economy went into free fall and jobs disappeared, many of them not to be seen again. Students emerged from commencement exercises with a diploma and a debt load that made them an instant credit risk and a burden for their parents or prospective mates.

We simply must find a way to make higher education more efficient and more affordable.

Consolidation is a logical place to begin.

THE PROMISE

The concept of higher education for everyone, with community colleges, state colleges, and universities, would remain intact but the horse-and-buggy constraints would go away. We're a highly mobile society now, so why remain wedded to the constraints that define so many of our institutions?

The University of Washington in Seattle has a world-class medical school that serves that state and aspiring physicians from Idaho, Wyoming, and Montana as well, sparing those three states the expense of building duplicate institutions. Why shouldn't, say, North and South Dakota, Iowa, and Minnesota find a way to conflate their medical schools so duplicative costs go down and resources are spread more evenly for more efficiency? Curiously, much of the resistance to the consolidation of schools and colleges is rooted in conservative rural areas where legislators and voters demand fiscal efficiency in every other form of government.

I have no illusions about the political difficulty of deconstructing what has been in place for so long. But if education is to be America's best offense and defense against global competition, hard, big, and bold choices have to be made.

Here are two realities that cut across all our hopes and expectations for improving education and its societal benefits in America.

Poverty: During the Great Recession, the number of homeless children exceeded one million. Almost one in five kids lived in households at or below the poverty level. Those are not conditions disconnected from fulfilling the promise of education. They have to be addressed as well.

School term: The time for the nine- or ten-month school term has come to an end. If American education is to measure up against global competition, time spent in the classroom or in some form of learning environment must be extended. In a society where more and more families have both parents working, we have a vast population of unsupervised kids disconnected from adult supervision and from the discipline of learning for two to three months a year. Education experts call that the "spring slide," when students, especially those in lower socioeconomic groups, lose a lot of what they learned during the academic year.

Nonetheless, the idea of extending the school term is not popular among parents. Most polls show the opposition running about two to one. A variety of reasons are offered, including interference with family vacations and the experience young people gain at summer camp or while working a summer job.

Here's a suggested start: Extend the school year to eleven months and make the eleventh month morning or afternoon only. For teenagers who need to earn income during the off-season, bring employers into the equation with tax credits for participating in work-study programs.

CHAPTER 5

Don't Know Much About Geometry

FACT: In China it is mandatory for all junior high students to study biology, chemistry, and physics; in the United States, only 18 percent of high school students take those courses.

QUESTION: Where have the most exciting and beneficial developments in our life come from in the last quarter century? From science, right? From computer mavens and biomedical whizzes, from energy engineers and environmental biologists.

The evidence is all around us, and success is not limited to the rock stars of that world— Steve Jobs, Mark Zuckerberg, or the Google boys, Sergey Brin and Larry Page.

Sitting in a New York University hospital waiting room recently, awaiting a routine checkup,

I picked up the NYU medical bulletin and read about Dr. Jan T. Vilcek.

Dr. Vilcek and his wife escaped to America from Communist-controlled Czechoslovakia in 1965, and he joined the NYU medical faculty. With a colleague he developed the popular anti-inflammatory drug Remicade.

His royalties were astronomical so he began a program of giving $100 million to NYU for research and medical education, explaining, "We decided to base the scholarships on merit rather than need because my goal is to improve the competitiveness of our medical school and attract the most highly qualified and talented students."

THE PAST

I wonder how Dr. Vilcek's vision would fit in with Ben Braddock's future?

Remember the scene in the celebrated 1967 Mike Nichols film **The Graduate,** in which Benjamin (Dustin Hoffman), a young man caught between the conventions of his fifties-era parents and the zeitgeist of the sixties, gets advice from Mr. McGuire, one of his father's friends?

"Plastics" was McGuire's laugh-out-loud key to the future.

If Mr. McGuire were confiding in Benjamin in this age of computers, digital phones, and desperately needed new energy sources, the dialogue might go like this:

McGuire: "I just want to say one word to you. Just one word."

Benjamin: "Yes, sir?"

McGuire: "Are you listening?"

Benjamin: "Yes, I am."

McGuire: "Science."

Science, not plastics, and if Benjamin were to continue, as he does in the film, by asking, "Exactly how do you mean?" I would hope even someone as intellectually constricted as McGuire would say, "Because, Benjamin, math, physics, science of all kinds, have always been important but never more so than now in this technological world. If you doubt me, visit a classroom in Singapore or Shanghai, Seoul or Mumbai."

THE PRESENT

Although exact numbers are difficult to come by, it's estimated China has at least 12 million students enrolled in core science curricula at institutions of higher learning. That does not include the Chinese students enrolled in America's best centers of high-tech education, students who will take those skills back home to help their native country move ahead of the nation that educated them.

During the 2008 Olympic Games in Beijing, I reported on China's leading computer science institute. It was run by a Taiwanese national, Andrew Chi-Chih Yao, who had been educated in the United States and had become one of America's leading authorities in computer education. He taught at MIT, Stanford, UC Berkeley, and Princeton before the Chinese government recruited him to run Tsinghua University, a prestigious technology academy training the country's best young minds in computer science.

Students who qualify arrive from throughout the country, for even in the rural areas the fundamentals of a broad range of sciences are required courses. Yao was thrilled with the quality of students he was attracting from all over China. His only concern was whether they would eventually succumb to the siren song of investment banking and venture capital instead of staying in the pure sciences. (We met just before the great American financial meltdown reached catastrophic proportions, a development that might have prompted some second thoughts about investment banking as a future.)

The result of China's commitment to science— both by the government and the wider population—

is the reason that bright, young Chinese economists visiting U.S. companies, think tanks, and academies give off a strong but unspoken impression. In tone and attitude they appear to be thinking, "We're coming and you're leaving."

In an **Atlantic** magazine essay on the future of America, journalist James Fallows welcomed that attitude, in context. "America will be better off if China flourishes than if it flounders," he argued. "A prospering China will mean a bigger world economy with more opportunities and probably less turmoil."

For now, however, China and India still have a long way to go to catch up. In universal aptitude tests, scholars at India's best institutions of science and math score in the lower half of the global universe of science students. Fallows notes that China's top science and technological institutions are not among the one hundred best in the world.

Other studies have turned up a quality gap between U.S.-trained engineers, for example, and those trained in India and China. In 2005, the McKinsey Global Institute determined that more than 80 percent of engineers educated in America were employable in the global economy. Only 10 percent of the Chinese trained in their country were ready for the demands of the global workplace. Indian engineers were more prepared, but they had serious shortcomings, such as the inability to think for themselves. They were oriented to follow orders, not innovate, according to several surveys.

Chinese science education has similar weaknesses. Creative thinking, entrepreneurship, and interpersonal and intercultural skills are not emphasized. In a book called **China's Emerging Technological Edge: Assessing the Role of High-End Talent,** authors Denis Fred Simon and Cong Cao concluded, "Chinese universities have become technique focused. . . . Rote learning, in which students who can answer questions in classrooms may not be able to solve and manage real life problems, still dominates higher education" there.

One prominent American businessman who has spent decades in China admires the country's enterprise and the turn it has taken in the past twenty-five years, but, he told me, "They still don't know what they don't know."

We cannot count on that disparity at the highest educational levels lasting forever. China and India are just beginning their national crusades for excellence and they both have a vast population of students eager to take advantage. They're beginning to recognize and address the issues of imaginative management and critical thinking at the computer console or on the high-tech assembly line.

Richard C. Levin, the president of Yale University, is convinced that China and India can catch up by the middle of the century. Writing in **Foreign Affairs** magazine, he cited China's commitment to establish its own Ivy League, what the Chinese call the C-9, and India's determination to build fourteen world-class universities.

Levin says the Chinese are ahead of India in getting beyond rote learning to critical thinking by developing more liberal educational institutions, but he raises the essential question: Can you have a world-class comprehensive university while constraining freedom of expression in political, social, and humanities studies?

In the end, Levin believes the rapid evolution of Chinese and Indian higher education is a force for good, concluding, "The fate of the planet depends on humanity's ability to collaborate across borders to solve society's most pressing problems—the persistence of poverty, the prevalence of disease, the proliferation of nuclear weapons, the shortage of fresh water and the danger of global warming. Having better-educated citizens and leaders can only help."

Yale is among the many educational institutions actively recruiting students from Asia and establishing new relationships. Levin connected with the University of Singapore to create a Yale liberal arts center in that tiny but powerful island state. It will be Singapore's first liberal arts college, offering what the two schools promise will be "education from the Western and Asian perspective."

It's not just the elites looking east. The Reformed Church in America, with its roots in Holland, has small colleges in Iowa and Michigan hoping to find new students through their network of Reformed Church missionaries in the Pacific states and Asian mainland.

The world is getting smaller, campus by campus.

In the meantime, the challenge for America is to make it easier for motivated students from wherever to come to the United States, the immigrant nation, for their education, and then to stay.

Not long ago, only about 10 percent of the Chinese who attained a doctorate in America returned home. Now, with the new opportunities in China, that percentage is moving up steadily and American immigration policies are contributing to the loss of the best and brightest from foreign lands.

Foreign nationals who want to stay typically end up with an H-1B visa, which limits their time in America to seven years before it can be renewed through a tedious process involving their employers or financial backers and the Immigration and Naturalization Service.

A few years ago a speaker at an Aspen Institute conference in Colorado came up with what all participants agreed was the single best idea to emerge from all the rhetorical ping-pong. He suggested having an immigration official stationed at every American graduation ceremony for science students. As the foreign graduates walked off the stage, the INS official would step up and staple green cards to their diplomas.

Susan Hockfield, the neuroscientist who became the first female president of the Massachusetts Institute of Technology, put the immigrant scientist equation in perspective in an op-ed column for **The Wall Street Journal.** "From MIT alone," she wrote, "foreign graduates have founded an estimated 2,340 active U.S. companies that employ over 100,000 people."

That's obviously a welcome dividend for America, but as Hockfield pointed out, "Amazingly, if as incoming students they had told U.S. immigration officials that they hoped to stay on as entrepreneurs after graduation, they would have been turned back at the border."

President Hockfield isn't the only opinion leader to recognize the disconnect between immigration policy and national needs. **New York Times** columnist Thomas Friedman, an articulate and imaginative champion of urgently upgrading America's science education standards, described attending a black-tie Washington dinner to honor finalists in the Intel Science Talent Search. The vast majority of the finalists, all American high school students, were from families that had immigrated here from India and China.

As Friedman wrote, these immigrant families are "the key to keeping us ahead of China. Because when you mix all these energetic, high-aspiring people with a democratic system and free markets, magic happens."

Friedman called the dinner the most inspiring experience he'd had in twenty years in Washington, and he wound up his column quoting the student spokesman for the group, Alice Wei Zhao of North High School in Sheboygan, Wisconsin. She told the audience, "Don't sweat the problems our generation will have to deal with. Believe me, our future is in good hands."

That is, if the grown-ups give the youngsters the tools and support they need.

True, students in mostly white suburban American schools hold their own against students in global math and science competitions, but we're not the United States of White Suburbs.

Fundamental math skills will be required at all levels of our society, as the requirements for workers evolve along ever more technological lines. It is no longer enough to have just a strong back, good hands, and a pair of sturdy boots to be a valued worker.

If, for example, Benjamin from **The Graduate**

followed Mr. McGuire's hypothetical twenty-first-century advice and pursued a career in which math and science skills were important, he might apply for a job at Google, the company that has spread its applications all over this new universe.

Benjamin would not be alone. It's estimated Google gets three thousand job applications a day through its website. Promising applicants are invited for an interview that, according to the company, "evaluates your core software engineering skills, including: coding, algorithm development, data structures, design patterns, analytical thinking skills. Interviewers will ask questions related to your area of interest and ask you to solve problems in real time. Creativity is important."

Google developer advocate Don Dodge, a twenty-year veteran of the tech industry who had worked at Microsoft, says he nonetheless was asked for his SAT scores and college grade point average when he applied for a position at Google. He was also asked to solve problems such as "There are eight balls. Seven of them weigh the same but one is heavier. Using a balance scale how do you find the heaviest ball in just two weighings?"

Other Google brain tests were more practical. "Say an advertiser makes ten cents every time someone clicks on their ad. Only twenty percent of the people who visit the site click on the ad. How many people need to visit the site for the advertiser to make twenty dollars?"

"If you had a million integers how would you sort them and how much memory would that consume?"

"What is the best and worst performance time for a hash tree and a binary search tree?"

"Write some code to find all permutations of the letters in a particular string."

Google attracted a lot of engineering applicants by posting a problem on a San Francisco–area billboard and inviting those solving it to apply for a job. The URL for the application process was hidden in the answer.

THE PROMISE

As one who has to refer to a calendar to remember his grandchildren's birthdates, I don't think I'd make it in a Google job interview. But I hope some of my grandkids might, once they get past their twenty-second birthday, whenever that is.

America's shameful record in creating a foundation of science-literate citizens is not a secret in the public or private sector.

Some of America's most successful entrepreneurs—Bill and Melinda Gates, hedge fund billionaire and former math professor Jim Simons, and billionaire California home builder Eli Broad—are devoting big chunks of their fortunes and personal energies to improving American education through innovative teaching programs and supplemental funding for school districts. But the popular culture works against them, despite the conspicuous success of former math and science whiz kids such as Gates, Jobs, Brin, Page, Zuckerberg, and Gordon Moore and Andy Grove of Intel. (Full disclosure: When I encountered advanced algebra and trigonometry, I knew my future would be more rewarding with words and political events than with x, y, and cosines.)

A few years ago in St. Louis I appeared before a group of journalism students at Washington University, a prestigious school with an enviable reputation in the sciences. The meeting took place in a chemistry lecture hall with a large display of the periodic table looming over the speaker's podium.

I began by staring at it for a moment and then gesturing as I said to the students, "That, ladies and gentlemen, is why I am journalist."

While the periodic table and I went our separate ways, one of my many informal rules of life is that those inclined to science are stimulating company with a wide range of interests. I never have a better time on a campus than when I visit Caltech or MIT,

Stanford or Johns Hopkins, because the students in the sciences combine the intellectual discipline of their fields with the curiosity of explorers in all they do, including their personal commitment to social causes.

James Trefil, a physics professor at George Mason University, has written that if we expect citizens to deal with the complex problems of global warming, stem cells, genetic engineering, food additives, and the like, "The very least we can do is teach them the basic principles that underlie the problem." Science is as critical to the making of a modern citizen as plowing with a team of horses was to the making of a successful nineteenth-century homesteader.

Education at an elite institution will not be the only ticket to employment in the new world order. In the evolving global economy there are going to be very good jobs for Americans willing to go abroad, not just for foreigners willing to come here. A graduate of, say, Colorado State University's College of Engineering who spends four years working in China's energy industry, picking up the language and getting to know the culture, adds real muscle to his or her résumé when it's time to come home.

I like to remind upscale parents that while they

fret over admission strategies for the Ivy League schools or any number of the elite institutions, the first choice for students in some parts of America, including in much of rural America, is enlisting in the Navy, Air Force, Marine Corps, or Army. The U.S. military is tough duty, but it's also a gateway to learning real skills or qualifying for college financial aid.

During a reporting trip on the USS **John C. Stennis,** one of America's nuclear-powered aircraft carriers, I was taken deep into that floating colossus to meet the young technicians who work 24/7 to maintain its high-tech components. The skills they learn there are readily transferable to a civil society in constant need of a workforce trained to keep our electronic homes, factories, offices, and public institutions humming.

Throughout the ship I saw earnest young sailors bent over their laptops, taking college courses or vocational training online. That was before passage of the Post-9/11 GI Bill, under which young men and women are now eligible for financial support for tuition, fees, books, and housing after ninety days of aggregate service or thirty days if discharged with a service-connected disability.

Democratic senator Jim Webb of Virginia, a highly decorated Marine veteran of Vietnam and a graduate of Georgetown University's law school, led the drive to expand the educational benefits for those currently in uniform, recognizing that the vast majority of men and women in the all-volunteer military are the underrepresented working-class young.

This is an investment that goes well beyond the young person who heretofore had little hope of getting a college degree or specialized vocational training. The presence of veterans on campuses or at select training schools is a major step toward addressing the disconnect between the 1 percent of Americans in uniform and in harm's way and the 99 percent of us who can go about our pleasurable civilian lives without even acknowledging wars are under way.

Washington University studied the gap between the uniformed military population and civilian society and concluded it represents a serious threat to the American polity because it could lead to a more politicized military, presumably because those in uniform believe they're either being ignored or are underappreciated by the civilian population. Furthermore, if those in uniform feel they're being ignored or undervalued, why bother joining in the first place?

On the campuses where they're enrolled in GI Bill programs, veterans do much more than remind their fellow students by their presence that the military is not incidental to American life. California State University chancellor Charles Reed says the veterans are "the exact profile of the kinds of students we want—smart, serious but balanced, committed, contributing and diverse."

Corporate America knows the value of military training and the disciplined, technologically based education that comes with it. General Electric is an enthusiastic recruiter of military officers in their late thirties or early forties who are captains, majors, or colonels. They've given their country fifteen or twenty years of their lives, and many have graduate degrees to go with their on-the-job training as personnel managers, problem solvers, and motivators. They arrive in the private sector with a can-do attitude and the chance for a second career that will take them into their fifties and sixties. In the modern parlance, that's called a win-win.

In a book called **Start-up Nation: The Story of Israel's Economic Miracle,** authors Dan Senor and Saul Singer studied the impact of mandatory military service for young Israelis on Israel's booming entrepreneurial economy and concluded that early training in the Israel Defense Forces was the critical component. Israelis go into the IDF right out of high school and quickly learn the values of teamwork, discipline, and, most of all, wise risk management.

Following their military service they enroll in college and continue their preparation for the daunting world of start-up businesses. They're mature beyond their years and Israel gets a twofer: a strong, all-inclusive commitment to national security and a post-military population equipped to take the economy to the next level.

The economic downturn did force one important change in post–high school education: Community colleges suddenly became popular destinations for the young who want a job but are not inclined to four-year higher education institutions.

From 2007 to 2008 enrollment at community colleges promising job training jumped 10 percent in the eighteen- to twenty-five-year-old demographic. And they're a bargain at under three thousand dollars a year on average.

More important, community colleges are rapidly expanding their capacity to train workers for the demands of the modern world. Gateway Community and Technical College just south of Cincinnati in Covington, Kentucky, is a model. The president of Gateway told me, "Twenty-five years ago eighty percent of the factory work was brawn, twenty percent brain. Today it is ten percent brawn, ninety percent brain."

Gateway Community was opened in September 2010 with the help of local manufacturers who desperately needed skilled younger workers to fill in behind a generation of workers trained on the job and now approaching retirement. It is a gleaming twenty-eight-million-dollar college with classrooms and a gymnasium-sized space filled with workstations to train students in electronic power systems, hydraulics, and pneumatics. A major part of the curriculum is problem solving, so the graduates emerge with much more than just a rote set of skills. They must have brains to match their manual dexterity to land jobs in local plants, such as MAG Industrial Automation Systems, once an old-fashioned tool and die company.

MAG is now part of a privately owned conglomerate turning out sophisticated elements for aerospace, automotive, mining, rail, wind, solar, oil, and gas industries around the world. Its local factory, about fifteen minutes from Gateway Community College, is a showcase for the modern age of manufacturing: precision mining tools, airplane fuselages, solar panels, fighter jet wings, and automotive gear boxes.

The brightly lit, quiet workspace shows off space-age, highly computerized machines as complex as the human nervous system. At each station workers in company-issued polo shirts manipulate them with their laptops open in a temperature-controlled, filtered air environment.

This is the leading edge of the evolution of American manufacturing, the high-tech business that can help redefine the new industrial age. It is a long way from the grimy, steel-on-steel tool and die origins of the factory when manual laborers were required to have only a strong back, good hands, and a tolerance for earsplitting noise, low light, and high temperatures.

MAG is on a desperate hunt for younger workers with the brains and skills to replace its graying employees headed for retirement, a generational shift so widespread it is called the "silver tsunami." In the middle of a long run of high unemployment, you'd think that would not be a problem. But it is.

Bill Horwarth, the athletically trim president of MAG, told me that too many of today's high school graduates are simply not prepared. "It's been a real struggle," he said, "to get the mechanical and electrical discipline we require to build the products we do."

As MAG's human resources officer Bill Weir puts it, "You can't find 'em. You can't steal 'em. You have to grow 'em." Gateway Community College is the nursery, and thirty-three-year-old Joe Snyder is one of the workers under the grow lights.

Snyder was an enterprising electrician who had a

small residential contracting company, the kind of work that has long been a fixture on the American landscape of housing developments and strip malls. Then came the Great Recession.

Joe's business dried up, but his skill set was a strong foundation to take him to the next level of worker competency. Besides, Joe had an uncle who was preparing to retire at the MAG plant.

Joe caught on as an apprentice at MAG with the proviso that he'd simultaneously enroll at Gateway Community College in their mechatronics program. As he told me on the MAG factory floor, "When I got here I thought I knew it all; three and a half years into it, I still don't know enough."

So after a full workday at MAG he shows up at Gateway for classes in hands-on electronics and problem solving. Gateway knows what he needs because as Dr. G. Edward Hughes, the school's president told me, "We're constantly checking with the employers so we can customize our training. We also get requests from them on how to adjust to what we're doing."

Joe is a perfect match for the Gateway program. The school has been able to place 80 percent of its graduates in good jobs, but I wonder about the future of two other men I saw laboring over an electronic circuit board at Gateway.

They were probably ten years older than Joe, and

they seemed to be struggling with the task at hand. One was an out-of-work truck driver and the other was a laid-off warehouse employee. They had been enrolled at Gateway for more than a year and still had no job prospects.

The figures are stark. The unemployment rate at the beginning of 2011 for those without a high school diploma was more than 15 percent. Workers with just a high school diploma represented the mean, at 9.8 percent. The unemployment rate for college degree workers was half that.

Age is a complicated issue in the national workforce. Forty percent of the members of the national workforce in 2009 were forty-five and older; that's almost a 100 percent increase in the share of older workers in the last quarter century.

Paradoxically, while older workers have a lower unemployment rate than their younger counterparts as a result of seniority on the job and the experience they bring to their positions, in the universe of the long-term unemployed, older workers represent the largest single group. Why? Seniority does you little good if your plant closes or your company goes out of business. Unemployed older workers have higher wage expectations, and hiring companies often want to start fresh at a lower salary.

As a result, long-term unemployment, twenty-seven weeks and more, hits the older worker the hardest. That rate is 37 to 40 percent among older workers, a further complication for a society already struggling with the prospects of elderly health care and entitlements.

Two Rutgers University professors in the fall of 2010 released a survey of workers not unlike those two Gateway students. The poll of eight hundred workers nationwide showed 14 percent of them had lost a full- or part-time job, and 73 percent of those questioned said either they or a family member or a friend had also lost a job.

Professor Carl Van Horn said the workers have "diminished expectations about America's economic future," a troubling reversal of the long-standing optimism of Americans who have always thought that things will get better. A majority of the workers in the Rutgers study believed the economy has undergone a fundamental change and will get worse.

Who can blame them? During the Great Recession companies learned they could get along with fewer employees. Those firms that did begin to hire again were able to get new workers at a lower starting wage than those they replaced. Pensions and other company-provided retirement benefits are under assault. Families, companies, and the government should start addressing these issues now in a realistic fashion so we don't end up midcentury with class warfare based on age.

Joe and his classmates represent an important change in attitude among male workers. They now know they can't take a job for granted and that their future depends much more on their reasoning skills than on their strong backs and a good pair of work boots. Still, nationally men make up less than 40 percent of community college enrollments. Women—both those in search of additional skills or career changes and mothers returning to the workplace—are now the dominant sex in the classroom, representing more than 60 percent of the community college enrollment nationwide.

Those women and their college-educated sisters are making a rapid ascent through the layers of America's workaday world. Women between the ages of twenty-five and thirty-four with a college degree can expect to earn a whopping 79 percent more annually than their generational sisters who finished high school only. Women with some post–high school education make 25 to 30 percent more than those with only a high school diploma.

Disparities in earnings between college- and high-school-educated people go well beyond purchasing power; these disparities affect their confidence and self-esteem as well.

In the 2010 midterm elections a representative cross section of voters were asked if they still believed in the American Dream, that fixed part of the American experience.

A stunning 40 percent said they had given up on what we've always assumed was a common goal. The one factor that separated the dreamers from the disenfranchised?

Money.

Those who had surrendered the dream, however they defined it, were earning as much as fifty-five thousand dollars a year, while those who still believed in the dream were making seventy-five thousand dollars and up annually.

The income and cultural gap between those with at least some higher education after high school and those without has been widening for the past three decades. As **New York Times** columnist David Brooks has commented, "In 1964 the educated and the less educated lived similar lives. Same divorce rates, same smoking rates. But since the rise of the Baby Boomers coincided with the importance of education, that has changed."

College-educated couples have half the divorce rate, half the obesity rate, and half the smoking rate, and they vote twice as often. When it comes to income, the differences are just as striking and perhaps more ominous, for if the money gap between the working class and the college educated continues to widen as dramatically as it has in

recent years, how long can it be before there is measureable class warfare, especially with the old safe-
guards of pensions and other social contracts
starting to fray? At a time when we need to be
strong at our weakest points to deal with global
competition, an economic civil war would be frat-
ricidal.

CHAPTER 6

Church of Thrift

FACT: In August 2010, total household debt in America equaled 121.7 percent of after-tax income. When the U.S. economy stagnated at the turn of the twenty-first century and job growth slowed, too many families who had gotten used to buying whatever they wanted whenever they wanted began to borrow in record proportions. We had gotten hooked on expensive cars, rooms full of new electronic toys, Las Vegas vacations, cruise lines, dining out, and the biggest buy of all, a house.

Add on the higher cost of health care and the cost of raising a child, not to mention exorbitant credit-card late fees, and it was a formula for washing the middle class in red ink.

QUESTION: When was the last time you had a family conversation about your short- and long-term financial goals? How much did you save last week? Do you know how much you put on your credit card before you receive the monthly bill?

Deep in my parents' closet, tucked away behind their modest wardrobes, was a small locked box with the family birth certificates, their marriage license, insurance policies, the passbooks for their savings account, and a stack of twenty-five-dollar war bonds.

The bonds, which paid a paltry 2.9 percent when cashed at maturity after ten years, helped finance America's astronomical costs for fighting in World War II. Yet they were phenomenally popular, largely as a result of a mass marketing campaign that featured Hollywood's biggest stars, including the GIs' favorite pinup, Rita Hayworth. War heroes were flown home to help with the effort. Three of the Marines who raised the flag on Iwo Jima were ordered by FDR to appear in Washington, D.C., at Major League Baseball games, and at a war bonds rally in Chicago that drew forty-five thousand people to Soldier Field.

By war's end, more than half the population had bought a war bond and raised almost $186 billion. Remember, the average annual family income at the time was two thousand dollars.

The bonds in my parents' closet had a kind of sacred quality in our family. They were one of the unspoken lessons of my youth: Save your money and help your country. When the United States went to war in Vietnam and later in Iraq and Afghanistan, there was no unifying financial sacrifice. They were wars financed on a credit card that had a big penalty for a late payment.

I thought about the small stash of Brokaw war bonds when in a White House briefing in early 2011 I heard the chairman of President Obama's Council of Economic Advisers say, "We have a national savings rate of less than zero."

THE PAST

There are so many stories about the calamitous collapse of the American economy in the Great Depression that it would be hard to settle on just one. I've heard my family's accounts of lost farms, dust storms, dime-an-hour jobs, and skimping on everything, always told as a matter-of-fact recitation of the realities. I grew up with those stories, but I cannot remember any anger or whining in their retelling.

A few years ago I was deeply impressed by the details in a book called **The Great Depression: A Diary,** published by the son of a Youngstown, Ohio, lawyer. The lawyer, Benjamin Roth, kept a meticulous journal of the day-to-day developments he witnessed and experienced.

His notes from several days in the fall and early winter of 1932 provide a stark accounting of the desperate times for ordinary Americans.

November 19, 1932

It seems unbelievable but conditions seem to be even worse. The month of October was the worst in my law practice but November is on the way to beat that low record. So far this month I have taken in $19 in cash. In the meanwhile the steel industry operates at 15 percent—bank failures start again last week with four in closing in Pittsburgh and five in Oklahoma.

December 1, 1932

Nothing new to report. Several hundred "hunger" marchers passed through Youngstown on their way to Washington where they will demand food instead of bullets when it [Congress] convenes Monday. I passed about two hundred of them . . . and they were singing the "Battle Hymn of the Republic."

December 5, 1932

A salesman just tried to sell me a small passbook on the Dollar Bank at 72 cents on the dollar. He states the tenants of the bank are using this means to pay their office rents, notes, mortgages, etc.

December 10, 1932

Business is at an absolute standstill. Merchants are fighting hard for Christmas business but report none is in sight. Last night's paper states that in Youngstown one out of every four families is being supported by charity.

By the end of the year, Roth noted that steel mills, the great engines of Youngstown's economy, were operating at just 13 percent of capacity; begging, holdups, and murders were frequent; and bankruptcies and foreclosures were no longer disgraces. The price of corn and wheat was so low—four and five cents a bushel—that farmers were burning their crops for heat rather than selling them for a loss.

Those conditions lasted across the country for most of the decade, imprinting a thrift gene on the people who lived through them. There was a common belief that it could happen again, a conditioning that stayed with this generation, and largely with their children, for the rest of their lives.

That thrift gene from the Depression was built into the bloodlines on all sides of our extended family. It had to be, for survival. The cost of living was not a statistic issued by a government economist. It was a daily reality.

Today, through marriage, we're the Brokaws, Conleys, Aulds, Harveys, Frys, and Bartfields and Simons. We have in our family albums cooks and butchers, farmers and city girls, garment workers and department store clerks, physicians and ranchers, football coaches and teachers, lawyers and community activists, journalists and businesswomen.

We're Huguenots, Irish, English, Scottish, Native Americans, and Russian Jews. All but the Simons and the Bartfields are rooted in the broad middle of the country, that swath of prairie and plains unfolding from the old Dakota Territory to the old Oklahoma Territory. The Simons and Bartfields are city folk; they got off the boat at Ellis Island in New York and never left.

We're a mix of high school graduates, college graduates, and elementary school dropouts. We are both working class and professionals. We're Republicans, Democrats, and independents, moderate to liberal, but none would be called radical or extreme. Some struck it rich while most stayed in the middle or working class.

The older ones were shaped but not broken by the Great Depression. The enforced economies of that long downturn stayed with them to the end of their days and gave them perspective when trouble emerged again from time to time.

My mother spent the first six years of her life living with her parents on a 160-acre farm in a one-room tar-papered "house." There was a loft where the hired hand slept surrounded by hams being cured, canned vegetables from the garden, and household tools.

The farm earned enough in the early twenties that the Conleys were able to build a small home with oak floors and two bedrooms but no indoor plumbing. Money ran out before they could paint the exterior.

Mother has only good memories of farm life despite the rustic conditions and absence of even the smallest luxuries. One year her favorite toy was a piece of a fence post she christened Maude and carried around as a make-believe friend.

Her education until the ninth grade took place in a one-room school. A precocious student, she listened in as the teacher worked with the older students and eventually skipped a grade.

A few years ago Mother was seated with Caltech president David Baltimore, a Nobel laureate, at a postgraduation luncheon in a campus garden. At one point I saw Dr. Baltimore listening intently to Mother explaining something. When I asked later what they were talking about, she said, "Well, I noticed in the tree nearby a Baltimore oriole and I pointed it out to him. I said, 'Look, there's the bird named after you.' He didn't seem to know much about them so I explained how they built a hanging nest."

In turn, I asked Mother how she knew enough

about the Baltimore oriole to be teaching a Nobel laureate. She said, "Oh, we learned all about birds and nature in that one-room school."

Life on the farm was instructive and rewarding in many ways, but when the boom years of the twenties ended and the twin evils of a great drought and a worldwide financial collapse ushered in the thirties, a hard life became even harder.

The Conley family lost the farm to the banks in 1931, forcing them to move to town, where my grandfather's new job at a local granary owned by a friend paid a dime an hour. Mother, a high school graduate at sixteen, gave up her dream of college and a career in journalism. She went to work as a postal clerk for a dollar a day, working nights as a waitress for fifty cents and her evening meal, called "supper" in rural America. She was invited by an aunt and uncle to live with them and try her luck in Minneapolis, where she found a job as a clerk for Fanny Farmer, the popular candy company with stores as ubiquitous in the Twin Cities as Starbucks outlets are now.

Fanny Farmer paid fifteen dollars a week, a tidy jump up from her South Dakota wages, and she had the added advantage of living with generous relatives. When I asked if she felt like the poor little country mouse in the big city, she said, "No, I felt rich. I had a job." Even with the job, however, she

When Mother moved to California her wardrobe became more stylish, but she didn't abandon her South Dakota thriftiness.

longed to return to northern South Dakota and her enterprising suitor, Anthony "Red" Brokaw, a third-grade dropout who nonetheless became a master operator of heavy construction machinery.

He could find work by racing hundreds of miles across the Midwest from highway jobs in Minnesota to new airports under construction in Kansas during the summer months. After they were married, he took Mother with him in a tiny homemade camping trailer. Occasionally they would rent rooms at boardinghouses. Like almost everyone else of their age they were thrifty by nature and by necessity. They didn't spend what they didn't have, and they saved something every week.

Now if I bring Mother the smallest gift during a visit to her comfortable retirement apartment—say, fresh-squeezed orange juice or roasted almonds—she asks how much it cost and then recites the price of every item she serves me for lunch. "Aren't those tomatoes nice? I got them for just a dollar ninety a pound, can you believe it?"

In an evocative memoir of life in Iowa during the Great Depression, author Mildred Armstrong Kalish writes in **Little Heathens** of the many ways of preparing basic farm food, or what I would call the Great Leftover School of Cooking.

Kalish asks, "What can you do with leftover mashed potatoes? Add beaten eggs, grated onions, and salt, form into patties like thick hamburgers, and fry them in bacon fat or oil until they are crispy and golden brown."

That was a staple at our family Monday night suppers, the mashed potatoes having been left over from the big Sunday noon dinner. My brothers and I liked to tease my mother by saying, "Oh, we're getting used potatoes again." It never failed to touch her off. "They're not used!" she'd exclaim. "They're as good as new."

Used potatoes didn't stay on my palate in my grown-up years, but I still have leftover guilt. I cannot easily discard still-edible food at the end of a meal, and as a result our refrigerator is a jumble of small containers of odds and ends. Leftovers were really a metaphor for the larger issues of money management and the ever-present fear that another Great Depression was just around the corner.

In our South Dakota hometown newspaper in the spring of 2009 there appeared an obituary for a woman born the same year as Mother. Blanche Horton worked in the Idaho potato fields for $1.50 a day during the thirties but, as the obituary noted, "one of her proudest achievements was saving enough money to buy a new ironing board which she used for the next 67 years."

I don't think Mother knew Blanche, but they shared more than an age. They were soul sisters in the church of thrift.

That instinct hasn't disappeared from our landscape. Recently in Montana I was fishing on a stream running close to a modest ranch. The proprietor is a widow in her seventies who lives in a small, plain house, surrounded by weathered corrals and a sagging machine shed. On the Sunday I was there she was busy with her brother and sister-in-law putting down new flooring in the kitchen. She'd gotten a good buy on some ready-to-install material at a local big-box supply store.

It was such a familiar scene for me, recalling those days and nights when I'd come home and my father would enlist me in some wiring, carpentry, painting, or roofing project. The idea of hiring outside help didn't cross his mind. Household appliances we now take for granted were cared for as if they were family jewels.

My New York son-in-law, Charles Simon, had a grandfather who could only afford an apartment so tiny that anyone leaning back in his or her chair at the kitchen table risked scratching the refrigerator door, and so the kids learned to always sit up straight rather than endure a shouted command to "Watch out for the refrigerator!" The entire apartment was three rooms. Charles's mother, Arlene, and her sister slept in the living room, and fifty years later she says those days of shared deprivation with so few material goods gave her a helpful perspective on life that remains with her to this day.

Charlie's father, Bruce, a prominent labor lawyer, grew up in the Coney Island environs, spending part of his childhood working for an uncle who was a popular fumigator. Bruce laughed when upscale Manhattan zip codes were hit with an infestation of bedbugs in 2010. "Too bad my uncle is not around; he had a homemade formula that really worked. I got twenty-five cents a mattress for applying it and I was probably just ten years old at the time." Bruce helped finance his law school education by working in a clam bar, and a half century later he's still a whiz at swiftly opening the tasty bivalves at our annual Thanksgiving gathering.

Allen Fry, my San Francisco son-in-law, grew up in small-town Oklahoma with grandparents who lived lives of self-reliance. His maternal grandfather, with only an eighth-grade education, went to work as a farmhand as a teenager and saved enough money to buy a thirteen-acre peach orchard that he converted into a small farm for himself, building a house and a barn from scratch without benefit of blueprints.

When Allen's grandmother graduated from high school she couldn't afford a class ring much less a college education, yet she found work as an insurance company secretary in nearby Tulsa, complementing her household chores with a passion for books.

Allen's great-grandfather was a Cherokee who landed in Oklahoma after traveling the Trail of Tears, Andrew Jackson's misguided attempt to solve the so-called Indian problem. Through marriage and births the family Cherokee lineage was reduced, but Allen's father retained his heritage as he became a celebrated Oklahoma schoolboy athlete and later a successful high school football coach and prominent citizen of Claremore, Oklahoma, the hometown of Will Rogers.

These lives, however differently they began and evolved, had a common theme: They were calibrated by prudent proportion. All of these men and women lived within their means, and they either intuitively or actively arranged their affairs so they could weather the unexpected.

They were also united by twin goals: that their children would have more prosperity than they did, and that they would achieve that by getting a college education. When the time came for their offspring to go to college, there would be money saved to pay the way or to help.

THE PRESENT

As a result, my generation on the family tree were the lucky branches when it came to realizing the American Dream: higher education, the economic opportunity that came with it, a more just society, and the advances of medicine and technology. Those are still the dreams today, but fewer of us are realizing the promise.

We came of age in the fifties when America was an unchallenged colossus economically. If you were a man, jobs were plentiful and many of them came with a generous package of benefits, including health care and pension plans. Women were still the victims of workplace discrimination, relegated to lower-paying jobs and constantly bumping against the now-famous glass ceiling. But they persisted and a combination of their skills, drive, and accomplishments opened the door wider for their daughters and other female members of the next generation.

We were the bridge generation, in a way, coming along as we did before the baby boomers. We were still conditioned by the penurious culture of our parents but a little giddy by what we were earning and all the new opportunities to spend. Dining out became routine. A second car? Why not? Let's fly, not drive, for vacation this year.

An all-purpose credit card was a major change in our lives. Meredith and I were in our late twenties before we got our first American Express card, which was the only one we carried. The idea of not paying cash for everything was uneasily liberating. It wasn't how I was raised.

There were some amusing moments as we drifted away from our parents' sensibilities.

My father went shopping with me at an upscale California food market and I thought I'd impress him by passing on the fresh-squeezed orange juice, noting that it was more expensive than the carton variety. He laughed, reached down into the shopping cart, and picked up three pricey bottles of California wine I'd selected without hesitation and said, "I guess the few cents you'll save on orange juice will pay for these."

CHAPTER 7

Survivors

> **FACT:** Between January 2007 and January 2011, an estimated nine million workers lost their jobs. An untold number of others took pay cuts, were furloughed, or started working only part-time.
>
> **QUESTION:** Do you have a contingency plan if you lose your job? Have you developed other skills or enrolled in some form of formal education that will prepare you for the demands of the rapidly changing workplace?

Dan and April Looper of New Vienna, in southern Ohio, were caught in the pincers of the economic downturn and the changing circumstances of their grandparents. The Loopers live in a rural area, in a four-bedroom house on two and a half acres with their four children not yet in their teens. In a way they would never have chosen for themselves, they became a poster family for the travails of America in the first great recession of the twenty-first century. (There will be others, for it is the inherent nature of large, complex economies to expand and then contract, whether from ill-advised free-market practices, misguided government policies, or natural disasters.)

THE PAST

Dan was one of eight thousand employees at Airborne Express, a branch of the shipping giant DHL, in Wilmington, Ohio. He went to work there right out of high school in 1998 and met April not long after. He had a good job as a trainer of new hires at Airborne, and so when they married she decided to become a stay-at-home mother, looking after the four children who followed in rapid succession.

The eldest, Alexis, has cerebral palsy and requires regular and expensive therapy. Dan and April were grateful for Dan's on-the-job health insurance, and they assumed it would be around as long as Dan's job, which, as he told me, he expected to last as long as he wanted it. "Airborne," he said, "was the one place that if anybody needed a job they could always go there. I honestly never thought I would see the day when such a big company would go under so quick."

He was stunned when in the summer of 2008 Airborne announced it would be shutting its Ohio plant within a year. Workers were offered early buy-outs, severance pay, and some benefits to tide them over until they could find other jobs. As a young father with a daughter who required extensive medical treatment, Dan didn't have that option.

Other, older men in his department, their families grown and on their own, stepped up and took early retirement so Dan could stay on the payroll for a year, a generous act that made a big impression on the Loopers. "They watched me grow as a dad and a husband," Dan said, "and they were watchin' out for me."

As grateful as they were for the temporary reprieve, Dan and April knew his day of reckoning would come within a year, and so they set out on a painful crash course in survival, their dreams of achieving middle-class standing deferred, maybe forever.

Dan spent his off-hours training as an EMT— emergency medical technician—and searching the Internet, looking for opportunities in what was an increasingly barren landscape for American workers with high school educations and few technology skills.

The Loopers cut up their credit cards. April says

that was the smartest thing they ever did after what she admits was a reckless start with the easy credit they offered. "We were dumb when we first got them," she said. "Really dumb, but we got smart and paid them off."

They started a regular savings schedule and trimmed their spending. But life intervenes, even when you have the best intentions. April sighs, "Then something will take us two steps back—the van breaks down or we gotta buy something for Alexis's therapy and the money we've been saving, well, now we have to use it."

THE PRESENT

April, a feisty redhead, shook her head and laughed as she described her new favorite shopping companion: coupons.

"Coupons are my favorite things," she said. "I used to see all those crazy ladies pushing shopping carts, flipping through the coupon books. Now I'm one of those crazy ladies, going down the aisle, flipping through the coupons.

"I used to buy the twelve-pack of batteries for kids' toys. Now when the toys go dead, they stay dead. I don't buy batteries."

April's and Dan's parents and grandparents have stepped up. "My grandma reminds me not to get down. She says, 'April, you just can't sit and sob because it will only get worse,' but then something will pop up with Alexis and we don't have money for groceries so I call my mom and say, 'Can you help us out?' Dan's mom has put gas in our car."

It's exhausting. "Wears me out is an understatement," April confessed with a tight smile. "Some mornings I don't want to get out of bed . . . because I have to face the fact of him losing his job and Alexis's health."

But she did keep getting up, and so did Dan. When Airborne moved its operations to Erlanger, Kentucky, a ninety-mile drive from their home, Dan was offered a job at the new location. Despite the long commute, he accepted.

After a year on the job in the new location, the future is looking a little brighter for the Loopers. "I worked my butt off and it paid off," Dan told me when I followed up with him nine months after our initial interview. "I got promoted to ramp supervisor in the loading operations, and in the winter I help supervise the deicing of the cargo planes."

THE PROMISE

On the phone, Dan had a new energy as he described how he and April were continuing to manage care-

The Looper family when their future was uncertain

fully. They've paid off both cars and refinanced their home so the payments are more manageable. "And April now buys two Sunday papers so she can get more coupons," he said.

Dan is making around fifty thousand dollars a year, which allows them to save more, and they're continuing to live by the rules that the recession first imposed on them.

When I asked about family entertainment these days, they jointly answered, "Watching the kids play in the backyard or turning on the garden hose and squirting them as they run past." Like so many couples hit by the recession, Dan and April rent inexpensive DVDs and watch them at home.

They also made room in their home for Dan's grandmother. "It was either that or a nursing home," Dan said. "We couldn't have that—so we took her in, and my dad paid for her food and drove her to her doctor's appointments and my uncle paid for her prescriptions."

Unfortunately, as so often happens, his grandmother's condition deteriorated to the point where she had to have constant care. Her move into a nursing home took a big emotional toll on the family. Dan's mother struggled with the reality that they could no longer take care of her themselves.

This is a story repeated in nearly every family across America as life spans are extended with the trade-off of commensurate physical and mental health difficulties. Care is expensive and often bewildering for family members who are forced to take responsibility for two lives: their own and their elderly relative's. Add dementia or Alzheimer's and it is a heartbreaking experience with too little relief.

Health-policy studies are warning of a coming cost crisis in long-term care for the elderly as more nursing home patients with dementia are using those facilities for longer periods of time. In 1999 patients with dementia averaged a stay of 46 days in hospice care with Medicare benefits. By 2006 that average had more than doubled to 118 days in hospice care. That's one more burden not just for families but for all taxpayers who are faced with the looming mathematical catastrophe of Medicare costs.

When I commented that the difficult times meant more elderly Americans were facing very tough choices and that Dan's grandmother was lucky to have a strong support structure, Dan responded matter-of-factly, "That's what families do—help each other."

CHAPTER 8

House Broken

FACT: In 1999, 1.2 percent of home loans were in foreclosure. The foreclosure rate stayed in that range until the housing bubble exploded. By 2009 foreclosure rates were running at 4.6 percent. Houses financed with high-risk sub-prime loans were foreclosed on at a rate of more than 15.5 percent. Experts have estimated 1.2 million homes could be repossessed by banks in 2011.

QUESTION: How much is your home really worth today? How much did you pay for it? Could you be just as happy in a smaller home?

At the close of the twentieth century America went through a housing speculation bubble that became our equivalent of Holland's tulip frenzy in the mid-1600s. Mortgages were ridiculously easy to get and the terms were ticking time bombs of a little cash down, interest-only payments for a few years, and then, boom, a very large bill due down the road.

In the fall of 2010, economists declared that the technical end to the Great Recession had come in July 2009, by their measurements, but that was little comfort to homeowners who had lost their homes or were struggling against the odds to hang on to property worth significantly less than what they paid for it. Banks and other lending institutions attempting to recover were also weighed down by permissive lending practices that became long-term obstacles to renewed financial health.

The fearsome reality of the depth and magnitude of the Great Recession began to catch America's middle class in the crosshairs. For several years wages for that section of the population had been in decline in real terms, or stagnating, while the cost of housing, education, food, and health care rocketed up.

The middle class began to borrow more, on their credit cards, at the bank, or on their homes. Too many of them made no commensurate cutback in their appetite for what television commercials, lifestyle magazines, and their neighbors assured them was the good life: a houseful of expensive appliances, dining out, long weekends at Walt Disney World or Las Vegas, leased SUVs, and late-model cars for the teenagers.

The great hope of breaking even by selling a

mortgaged home for much more than the initial investment disappeared overnight. Housing prices took a sharp turn downward at the peak of their inflated value, and as late as 2010 more than a quarter of homeowners in America were stuck with mortgages greater than the value of their house.

When the bubble burst, it set off a chain reaction that nearly led to a global depression.

As the economy struggled to recover going into the autumn of 2011, fueling an incendiary political debate, housing in America remained a primary problem.

The numbers were staggering: by the end of July 2011, banks owned but were unable to sell almost eight hundred thousand foreclosed homes and were in the process of foreclosing on another eight hundred thousand residential properties.

From the start of the recession in December 2007 through the summer of 2011, banks either foreclosed on or started foreclosure proceedings on approximately ten million homes, according to RealtyTrac, a national housing survey service.

THE PAST

A few years ago Meredith and I organized an informal reunion of South Dakota friends at our Montana ranch. We also invited a wealthy, politically and culturally prominent New York family. Only partly in jest I said to our New York friends, "This is a full-service group. One of the men is the chief federal judge in South Dakota. One of the women is a state supreme court justice; her husband is the former South Dakota attorney general. Two of the women are successful lawyers; the husband of one is now a college astronomy professor after retiring as one of the state's most successful high school football coaches. There at the end of the table with the World Series ring is a longtime friend who played second base for those championship Oakland A's teams in the seventies, and next to him is the proprietor of the busiest restaurant in our hometown."

I closed by saying, "They have two things in common: They're all successful and they all grew up in small towns, on farms, or on ranches in modest houses with one bathroom."

The federal judge corrected me. "We didn't have an indoor bathroom on the farm until I was a teenager."

It was good for a laugh, and then we had a lively dinner discussion with no discernible differences between the New Yorkers and the South Dakotans when it came to familiarity or insights on the big issues of the day.

The evening was, in its own way, a metaphor for the contraction of class differences on many levels in America. It was also a reminder of the expensive expansion in home construction in the recent past, and the diminished expectations of the present and future.

The increasing size of the family home and the rising ownership of second homes seemed to have happened with little commentary or examination. There may not be a more telling example of the differences in spending habits than the housing model. In the 1950s and early '60s, the Rocky Mountain ski areas were quaint villages; they erupted into glossy sprawls of trophy homes and condos. Florida coastlines and Arizona and California deserts blossomed with sun-dappled expensive weekend and winter housing. In every state, second homes morphed from rudimentary cabins on lakes and rivers to residences a huge percentage of the world's population would consider palaces.

My father-in-law was a successful physician in our hometown of Yankton, a thriving rural medical center in South Dakota. He built for his family of five children what the community considered to be at the time an impressive brick home with four bedrooms, three bathrooms, a small den, a "rec room" in the basement, a comfortable living room, and a two-car garage with a station wagon in one bay and a late-model sedan in the other.

The square footage of the entire house was probably about twenty-five hundred. That was a substantial symbol of real prosperity in the fifties and early sixties. Today Yankton has whole neighborhoods of homes a third again as large. The nearby lakeshore is laced with second homes, equal in size to or larger than Doc Auld's brick house on West Eighth Street.

The summer Meredith and I were married, 1962, the only second home on the lake I knew of belonged to the local banker. It was a small, modestly furnished cabin, but in its understated way it separated the banking family from the rest of us financially.

Dr. Auld and the banker had the means to build something much grander for their families, but modesty and proportion—not showing off—was an unspoken rule. When Doc bought two productive farms nearby, there was no resentment; that made sense. But if he had built what came to be called a McMansion, the community would have collectively wondered what had happened to the man they thought they knew.

The Brokaw family home during my teenage years was a two-story, three-bedroom house on a corner lot with an attached two-car garage that doubled as my father's mechanical workshop. It was the first house my parents purchased after twenty years of marriage spent living in small mobile homes, rented apartments, and government housing on U.S. Army bases and Corps of Engineers construction sites along the Missouri River.

Even though I was just fifteen when they bought the turquoise-colored home at 1515 Mulberry in Yankton, I was impressed by the purchase price: $11,500. It seemed a princely sum, but Mother later told me they had saved so much during the postwar construction boom that they could have paid cash.

Although the rooms were small—the bedrooms were, maybe, eight by ten feet—and there was only one bathroom for a family of three boys and Mother and Dad, it had a solid working-class respectability about it.

It was, as our visiting relatives would say, "a nice house."

When Meredith and I bought our first home in California in 1968, I was making around forty thousand dollars a year as a local anchor and network correspondent for the NBC-owned station in Los Angeles.

The house, a forty-year-old custom-built home in the hills above Studio City in the San Fernando

Valley, had three bedrooms and one bath at one end with a spare bedroom and another bath at the far end. In between there was a modern but not fancy kitchen, a sunny dining area, a small television room, and a living room with hand-hewn beams in the ceiling and a fireplace in the corner. It was in the fourteen-hundred-square-feet range.

I took time off from work to refinish a second-hand crib for our third child, steam old wallpaper off a bedroom wall, and paint a bathroom while Meredith spent a thousand dollars on handsome matching sofas and an expansive glass coffee table to place in front of the large picture window overlooking the valley.

Our small yard on a steeply pitched lot contained flourishing peach and lemon trees and an ivy-covered terrace. A stand of eucalyptus trees out back bordered a three-hundred-acre piece of county land off-limits to development. In that county tract there were deer, coyotes, hiking trails, and trees to climb.

We were surrounded by houses with pools in our woodsy cul-de-sac, and most of the neighbors were generous with invitations.

In short, for a pair of twenty-eight-year-olds from the prairie just starting a family, it was California bliss. Not for a moment did we feel house poor. For the next five years we entertained neighbors and friends, movie and television stars, presidential candidates, local politicians, famous athletes, and business moguls at casual Saturday and Sunday night dinners.

The house cost $42,500, just slightly more than my annual salary.

I occasionally drive up the narrow street on which it sat when I return to Los Angeles. I can no longer see our little nest from the street because someone has converted it into a gated mansion with an elaborate steel and concrete deck over what was once the ivy-covered terrace. I have no idea what the current value might be, but it must be at least two or three million dollars.

The reconstruction looks very expensive, but it appears to have turned out well. I hope the happiness we left behind wasn't lost in the conversion.

A good contrast between the standards of yesterday and today in the house-buying business is Graceland, Elvis Presley's celebrated estate on the outskirts of Memphis. It is one of the most popular tourist attractions in the Southeast and for members of my generation, it has a Shangri-La-like reputation.

Elvis, our poor-boy rockabilly icon, could rise up from his Mississippi shanty roots and buy a grand home. He purchased it in 1957, when just about everything Elvis did was breathlessly reported, and this was well before **Entertainment Tonight** or any of the other cable entertainment shows.

Graceland became more mythical once Elvis died. Paul Simon recorded a monster hit about going there, called "Graceland," which appears on the album of the same name.

So when I finally made my own pilgrimage a few years ago I half expected the grounds to have a kind of celestial feel and the home itself to be more castle than house. It is, it turns out, a period piece, stately but more modest in scale and statement than any number of homes on any number of streets in the moneyed neighborhoods of, say, Atlanta, Houston, Minneapolis, Seattle, or Boston. Graceland is a little more than ten thousand square feet over all, and yet Meredith and I were surprised to discover the living and dining rooms were about the size of those you'd find in large modern homes so popular with the upper middle class today.

At the time he bought it, Elvis was a huge star, the biggest recording artist on the planet, well on his way to becoming the legend that lives on. He bought Graceland for $102,500, and that included almost fourteen acres of land.

The terms? The king paid $10,000 down in cash, plus another $55,000 he received from the sale of the house his parents were living in. He took out a

$35,700 mortgage for the balance, payable over twenty-five years.

This kind of proportionate house pricing went on for another twenty years.

THE PRESENT

When it came time for our three children to find homes, they were at the wrong end of the great American real estate boom and living in two of the priciest cities in the country, New York and San Francisco. With our help, they each bought comfortable but not luxurious homes for prices that were, as I liked to remind them (not entirely in jest), what I once had hoped to earn in a lifetime of labor.

The big jump in housing prices has not been confined to big cities. Nationally, the median price of a new single-family home went from just over $160,000 in 1999 to $248,000 in 2007, a jump of more than 50 percent. The sale prices of existing homes went up close to 60 percent during that period.

It was a booming bubble until it wasn't, and then the landscape was littered with foreclosures, abandoned homes, unfinished developments, and failed lending institutions.

Owning a home and paying the mortgage that comes with it went from being the American Dream to worse than a nightmare for many families. Nightmares go away, but the consequences of owning a home worth less than you paid for it—foreclosure and credit difficulties—linger for a long while.

Our youngest daughter, Sarah, is not married and has no children, so the housing and economic strain on her is not as great, for now. But she's watched her sisters, and she knows the financial pressures that come with a family these days. As our San Francisco daughter, Jennifer, laments from time to time, she and her husband are both highly trained physicians in thriving practices but their finances are constantly strained by the cost of housing and education for their children. They turned to the private school option only after their daughters, Claire and Meredith, didn't win a place in the San Francisco public school lottery. They hope that San Francisco's public education standards will not wither under the strain of the city's and state's fiscal pressures.

Our New York daughter, Andrea, her husband, Charles, and their two daughters have an identical dilemma with the cost of housing and education. He's a Yale graduate with a law degree from the University of Chicago who has held senior positions in the Clinton administration Justice Department and the New York State Division of Criminal Justice Services. She has a senior management position at Warner Records.

They live in his old neighborhood, a collection of vintage apartments on the Upper West Side of New York. Not so long ago a couple with their résumés and earning power could have easily bought one of the apartments with their salaries. Now, as my daughter says, with a kind of morbid laugh, "Dad, I need to cash in before you check out."

This is not what our daughters expected when they left home to study at good universities. They had grown up in comfortable circumstances but always with the reminder of their grandparents' prudent lifestyle and constant admonitions from their parents that they were not trust-fund kids, inoculated against finding a working profession and pursuing it.

It is not that Meredith and I and our daughters are whining about all this. "Astonished" is a more apt description: astonished and concerned for those of their generation who aren't able to fill the gaps between income and the fundamentals.

This is, or should be, a lesson for our time—for all of us—whatever our financial status.

Shannon Oliver and her family were typical of what was going on.

I met them while crossing the country on U.S. Highway 50, reporting on the American character for USA, the cable channel. The Olivers personified the distressed population in Fernley, Nevada, a shake and bake suburb of Reno with rows of houses in new developments with names such as Ponderosa, Green Valley Estates, Autumn Glen, and Rawhide. If it was not the foreclosure capital of America, it was a contender.

Shannon was fighting to save their home, a modest modular house they had purchased in 2005 for $187,000, at a time when her construction worker husband Troy was making close to a hundred thousand a year in the building boom of northern Nevada.

They had moved from California to Nevada to find the good life and, as Shannon put it, "get the American Dream—our own home." But they wanted more, and why not? Didn't everyone they saw on their street or on television have more? So they bought two new cars as well. Shannon's eyes sparkle as she says, "I loved my little Jeep Liberty."

Making ends meet was a stretch but when Troy came home with extra pay from working overtime, it was reason enough to splurge on dinner and a movie out. Saving the overtime pay didn't occur to the Olivers.

Then it all came apart. The building boom went bust and Troy lost his job, and then another. Shannon drove a school bus but her salary was not nearly enough to keep up with their obligations. The cars were repossessed. The value of their home went into free fall, dropping to $60,000, in a neighborhood of foreclosures and desertions by others in similar straits. The Olivers' home was a modular unit, and today it is hard to imagine it ever had the real value of the original purchase price.

When we met in the fall of 2009, the Olivers' every waking moment was consumed by trying to find a way to save their home and what little was left of their dream. Shannon was reading everything she could find about government mortgage help programs and talking to her bank contacts, explaining that they could pay $950 on their mortgage but not the $1,500 called for in the contract.

Nothing worked. They simply had far too much debt and were eventually forced to declare personal bankruptcy. Even if they had been able to make a deal with the bank, their burden would not have been eased. A year later, a matching modular home in the same neighborhood was on the market for $49,000. By November 2010, Fernley, a community of just under 13,000 residents, had 530 homes in foreclosure, and prices continued to drop.

Still, Shannon, ever the optimist, saw a bright side. "We're spending more time together as a family," she said. Entertainment now is watching their son, Jayce, play football, or renting DVDs for a dollar a night.

"We've learned a very hard lesson," Shannon said. "We as a nation were living much too hard, much too big. We have to get back to basics."

Jayce often asks why they can't have the things they did before and Shannon has been patient in explaining the realities of their new economic condition. He's a serious nine-year-old and there's been little whining. When Jayce gets to his parents' age, how will he manage his finances after this searing experience of his childhood?

Perhaps he will be more mindful of saving before spending. There is no doubt he is getting an up-close look at the importance of education in developing job skills that improve your chances of working even when a recession comes along.

THE PROMISE

Marketing and retail research organizations are doing extensive work with young consumers to determine their current and future buying habits. One company, GTR Consulting, has already come up with a new name for them: neo-frugalists. The Food Institute commissioned a study on teenage eating habits during the recent economic difficul-

Shannon and Troy Oliver in the home they lost

ties and discovered there was a 20 percent drop in dining out for the younger set between the fall of 2007 and 2009.

A friend of mine, Doug Tompkins, had a turn-around moment in his life. With his former wife, Susie, he founded Esprit, the hip clothing company of the eighties and nineties. They became wealthy and bought a stunning home just off Lombard Street in San Francisco, which they filled with masterpieces from the Colombian artist Fernando Botero.

But then Doug, a world-class kayaker, rock climber, and deeply committed environmentalist, hit a philosophical conundrum: How could he be true to his environmental values and still push more clothing on consumers—more clothing than any-one could need?

"I asked my mom," he said, "how many shirts Dad had during the forties, and how many dresses she had. She said, 'Oh, I don't know—just a few.' That got me to thinking. 'Why do we need more now?' "

So Doug sold his interest in Esprit, sold much of his art, and moved to South America where he began buying up hundreds of thousands of acres in Chile and Argentina, converting them to wilder-ness parks or running them as sustainable ranches. As rich as he was at Esprit, he's even richer now, personally and financially.

———

Kevin and Joan Salwen of Atlanta have gotten a good deal of attention for a do-over of their lives prompted by a question from their daughter, Hannah. They were at a stoplight when Hannah noticed a homeless man with a sign saying he was hungry. There was a Mercedes at the same light, and Hannah said, "If that man had a less nice car, that [other] man could have a meal."

When the Salwens got to their two-million-dollar home in an upscale Atlanta neighborhood, the conversation continued about "How much is too much?" Hannah and her brother, Joseph, made it clear they didn't need all the things their parents' financial success could afford.

Kevin had been a **Wall Street Journal** reporter before becoming a successful entrepreneur and Joan was an executive at Accenture, the financial services firm, before returning to teaching, something she loved more.

The family dialogue didn't let up, and the Salwens came to a consensus: Let's sell this big house and give half to charity. The half amounted to $885,000 net.

They performed a diligent search of where they wanted the money to go and decided to spread it throughout twenty villages in Ghana. That, in turn,

Doug Tompkins, founder of The North Face
and Esprit, a world-class outdoorsman and
dedicated environmental philanthropist

led to a widely praised book, **The Power of Half: One Family's Decision to Stop Taking and Start Giving Back**, addressing what well-off families can do with half their home values or, carried to the extreme, their net worth.

As Kevin puts it, "Now we always look at our lives and the other halves we can do. We're always going to be involved."

Obviously, Tompkins and the Salwens are exceptions, even at the high end of the personal wealth scale.

The rest of us can be be inspired by their model, however, and pause to reflect on the large posters now adorning the lobbies of JPMorgan Chase, the nation's most successful large bank. They feature self-confident young men and women with the banner headline SAVE IS THE NEW SPEND.

Save for a smaller, more affordable home, perhaps. Obviously, the long-running trends have come to a halt. The average size of an American house expanded by 140 percent between 1950 and 2007, from just under 1,000 square feet to more than 2,400 square feet. That's twice the average size of homes in France and Germany.

Already, there are signs of a reversal. **The Wall Street Journal** profiled an Atlanta company, John Wieland Homes and Neighborhoods, that was known for building trophy homes throughout the

Southeast selling for an average of $650,000 apiece. Just a few years ago, they had Jacuzzis, butlers' pantries, vaulted ceilings over breakfast nooks, and laundry rooms as large as bedrooms. Now Wieland is building homes without fireplaces and substituting fiberglass tubs for the pricier tiled models.

One of Wieland's new homeowners spoke for many when he said, "There's a lot more that comes with those McMansions. There's a lot more cleaning, a lot more heating, a lot more cooling." There's also a lot more debt.

Opportunities could grow out of this dislocation between finances and fundamentals. For example, smaller, more energy-efficient homes in communities or developments with more green space could take the place of that third stall in a three-car garage. Urban dwellers seem to get along fine by sharing a common wall with a neighbor in an apartment. Why can't a new generation of suburbanites look to more townhouse construction with the saved energy costs of common walls and wider common green spaces in the neighborhood?

Many of the new homes in the New Orleans flood zones are getting high praise for their stylish design, energy efficiency, and a scale that adds up to a sense of cozy community.

If you Google "house size in America" you'll find not only statistics on square footage but also testimonies on the benefits of smaller homes from their owners in the comments section: "We may have the smallest home on our street but we're also the only ones who can afford to take nice vacations."

Call them what you will—McMansions, Hummer Homes, Garage Mahals—they are on their way out. Someday there may be an exhibit in the Smithsonian of how a popular trend in home building gave way to smarter ideas, such as energy efficiency and coziness.

In Marin County, California, Aspen, Colorado, and other communities where big money was put on display on ever larger homes, local officials are now putting a cap on construction size. A popular builder in Westchester County, New York, the affluent suburban area north of Manhattan, is getting work from investors who are swooping in to buy foreclosed McMansions and hiring him to downsize the homes by knocking off a wing or reducing the garage area.

Other communities are requiring remodeled homes or new construction to include a certification of green standards, indicating energy efficiency and the use of recycled materials. That is a harbinger of new construction codes that will become routine before too long, just as earlier regulations were updated to improve fire safety and earthquake resistance.

A Make It Right Foundation home in the
New Orleans flood zone—part of a
Brad Pitt project

As we emerge from the great downturn we'll get a better picture of the lasting effects of the mortgage meltdown on succeeding generations beyond pricing and borrowing capacity. If Americans once again rush out to buy more than they can afford or pay too little attention to home proportions and energy efficiency, it could be an ominous sign of lessons missed and a forerunner of other disappointments to come.

Owning your own home has always been central to the American Dream, but until the era of subprime loans and speculation frenzy as lenders, promoters, and developers baited the landscape with condominiums and freestanding homes at inflated prices, it was a deliberative process. Qualifying for a loan was not easy, and the decision whether to buy was carefully thought out. If we return to those fundamental values, the dream can be renewed. In the meantime, for many in the marketplace there is only one viable choice: rent.

That does not mean the idea or the reality of home ownership should disappear. When it began to be realized on a wide scale following World War II, starter homes were small and affordable, sized to match the expanding economy and the financial aid package available for veterans. It was the beginning of suburban America, new houses, neat lawns, and white picket fences. Visit any

American suburb today and measure the changes—
they are testimony to the changing definition of
that part of the American Dream. For those who
can financially manage it, "home sweet home" is
central to the idea of a successful life.

For those who cannot—those who become hostage to the pressures of their mortgage—the dream
becomes a nightmare and their homes become a
measure of a stressful life, not a successful one.

PART TWO

Assignment America

CHAPTER 9

Uncle Sam Needs Us

FACT: One percent of Americans wear a military uniform. They carry the battle for the other 99 percent of us, and nothing is asked of us in return.

QUESTION: Do you know anyone in the armed forces? Have you been in touch with a returning veteran or a veteran's family? Have you supported a military aid organization?

THE PAST

"Ask not what your country can do for you . . ."

On January 20, 1961, John F. Kennedy famously appealed to the nation he was about to lead to continue the ethos of his generation: "Ask what you can do for your country."

The young president ignited a fresh fervor for public service as the Peace Corps became the hot new destination for the young. It was followed by the stirring oratory of Martin Luther King, Jr., calling on all Americans to confront the deeply unjust and immoral reality of codified and de facto racial discrimination.

The U.S. armed forces were the primary form of public service in America until the war in Vietnam, which deeply divided the country. The United States discontinued the draft in 1973. The resulting all-volunteer military is today drawn largely from the working and middle class of the country.

We became two societies with too little connective tissue.

THE PRESENT

It is time to find a framework for national service that goes beyond a military uniform and provides a long-term benefit for the country. It is fundamentally unfair to expect a small percentage of our population, drawn largely from the middle and working class or poor, to carry the burden and pay the price of fighting wars that are always initiated in "the national interest," however credible or contrived the threat.

It took a while, but a number of civilian organizations eventually emerged to support the troops in the Iraq and Afghanistan wars, many of them providing crucial support to wounded vets and their families. Nonetheless, it remains a random exercise, and all the "Welcome Home" committees at airports are not a substitute for what should be, in a democratic republic, an organic relationship between a civil society and its military.

Not too far from wherever we are gathered, there are military families sitting by the phone hoping it doesn't ring with unbearable news. Annette Kuyper, one of the featured speakers at the 2010 dinner of the Minnesota Military Appreciation Foundation in St. Paul and the mother of a National Guardsman who served a year in Iraq, took the audience inside a mother's fear. While her son was away, Annette said, she closed the blinds on the windows that overlooked her driveway because she didn't want to see the arrival of a military vehicle carrying a National Guard chaplain with a dreadful message.

When her son did come home after an extended deployment, Annette said, his two-year-old daughter didn't recognize him and was tearful in his presence for several months. He had not been married long when he left for Iraq, so he and his wife had to restart their relationship, a task made more difficult by his conditioning from living an all-male environment in a combat zone.

The least the rest of us can do as fellow citizens

and the beneficiaries of their sacrifices is to find a way to connect to those families and ask, "How can I help?"

Corey Briest is a heartening example of what can go right when everything goes wrong in combat and the personification of just how much help these wounded veterans require. Corey went to Iraq at the age of twenty-four in 2005 as part of Charlie Battery, First Battalion, of the 147th Field Artillery, the National Guard in my hometown of Yankton, South Dakota. He had been working days in a small manufacturing plant and spending many of his nights as an emergency medical technician in Yankton, responding to tornado damage, car wrecks, and fires in that small city tucked along the Missouri River.

His wife, Jennifer, says, "Corey loved being an EMT and being in the National Guard," which he joined when he was seventeen. He also loved Jennifer, a special education teacher, and their two children, Kylie and Connor. By coincidence, they lived in a small, neat home my mother and father built when the Brokaw boys left home.

Jennifer and Corey's mother, Diane, were anxious when the Yankton Guard was deployed to Baghdad to help train Iraqi troops as security forces, but they kept in touch with Corey by email. All seemed to be going well until December 4, 2006.

Corey was riding in the gun turret of a Humvee in a caravan through Baghdad when first one and then two improvised explosive devices—IEDs—tore through the column.

Two of Corey's buddies were killed immediately, and a third died later. Corey, who had been responding to the first IED attack in his role as a medic, was grievously wounded by shrapnel piercing his brain. He became the latest victim of TBI, traumatic brain injury.

Back in Yankton, Jenny was preparing dinner for their two children when, she said, "The phone rang and someone from the Pentagon—I guess they were reading from a computer screen—said, 'Your husband has been bombed.' That's what they said! I thought it was some kind of cruel joke. They didn't have any more information."

Corey's mother was not home at the time so the Pentagon left a message on Diane's phone that her son had been badly wounded. It was the beginning of a long, often confusing, and always painful ordeal.

Corey was medevaced to Germany and then on to the National Naval Medical Center in Bethesda, Maryland, where Jenny and Diane flew to his side. The prognosis was so grim they began planning his funeral as he lay swaddled in bandages the length of his swollen body, breathing through a ventilator.

But then doctors noticed some encouraging signs in his brain activity, and they recommended a transfer to a Veterans Administration rehabilitation center in Minneapolis.

Corey continued to make some progress, but his Minneapolis physicians thought his recovery would be limited. They advised Jennifer to prepare to have him assigned to a nursing home for the rest of his days. "No way!" Jenny thought.

She concluded that the Minneapolis facility was simply overwhelmed by the continuing carnage of the two wars. Traumatic brain injuries are, in the clinical verbiage of Pentagon medical officials, "the signature wound of these conflicts."

So Jenny scoured the Internet. Through the website of another TBI veteran she learned of a private facility in Southern California called Casa Colina. The government was willing to transfer Corey there and pay the $21,000-a-month costs.

Jenny and Diane accompanied Corey to California and stayed with him for a year of intensive therapy and rehabilitation. It paid off. He learned to walk again, in a limited fashion, and to speak in a guttural tone that Jenny could understand. He was still blind and he'd never fully recover, but he was ready for what Jenny and Corey both wanted: to return to Yankton and his family.

Yankton was eager to have him back, but there

were so many questions: Where could he live? How would he get around? Could he ever work again? The publisher of the local newspaper called me looking for help, and I immediately suggested creating a 501(c)(3) fund so contributions would be tax deductible. When I offered financial assistance from the Brokaw family, the publisher called back to say the community was grateful but it needed to step up to help Corey as well, and so we agreed on a shared fund for housing and a wheelchair-accessible van.

South Dakota building contractors came through with Operation Opening Doors, a program organized by the Associated General Contractors of America to provide renovated or entirely new homes for severely wounded veterans. Operation Opening Doors raised $230,000 from local sources for the new Briest home, which would include an elevator and handrails everywhere to help with Corey's mobility.

When Jenny brought Corey home from California, a local organization called Bringing Sergeant Corey Briest Home turned out a large flag-waving crowd at the small municipal airport and escorted him to an even larger reception at the civic center, where he was awarded the Purple Heart and a Bronze Star.

Corey has been back in Yankton for almost five

years now and Jenny says they couldn't "be in a better place. Everywhere we go people stop to ask how we're doing, and Corey's buddies pick him up and take him to EMT meetings." Still, some of his old friends no longer come by, and when Jenny presses them for an explanation, they say, "It's too hard to see him that way and to try to communicate with him."

Too hard for them?

THE PROMISE

Jenny has become an advocate for other wounded veterans, writing regularly on a website called CaringBridge, an information center for families with members who are struggling with war wounds, cancer, or other debilitating conditions. In a cheerful tone she describes shopping trips to Walmart, or Corey helping the children with a bubble bath, all of which underscores her strong belief that the Pentagon and the VA have to place more emphasis on the whole family of wounded veterans.

"Remember," she told me, "I have to be in charge of the constant changes in his care from year to year to year. They worry primarily about his immediate care or just his hospital stay."

Then she brightens when she describes their now

twice annual trips to Colorado, where Corey has become a regular in a program called Challenge Aspen, which offers a recreational opportunity for wounded vets. "It's awesome," Jenny said. "Corey has been white-water rafting and skiing two years now and he loves it." In a photograph on the Challenge Aspen website there are Jenny and Corey with two other couples, the guys with baseball caps, broken bodies in wheelchairs, giving the thumbs-up sign, as their young wives tenderly embrace them.

When Corey came to a lecture I gave on the University of South Dakota campus in the fall of 2010 I was encouraged by the progress he was making with his speech clarity, and so I asked a family friend, "How's his vision?" She answered with a laugh, "Oh, it's improving, too. He likes to say he can see hot girls and cool cars."

When I visited the Briests at their home Jenny was quick to point out that Corey seldom uses the elevator anymore. "He works his way down that wide staircase to the family room," hanging on to the handrails on either side, she told me.

They enjoy watching movies together, Jenny explaining to Corey what he's missing visually as he listens to the dialogue. His daughter, Kylie, reads stories to him—a reversal of the father-daughter role he hopes someday to change. Since Kylie is nine, he figures he has time to work on his walking so he can accompany her down the aisle on her wedding day.

When I think about the support the Briests get back home, I am reminded of other young couples in working- and middle-class communities for whom the price of their service will go on forever. They're part of our common heritage, and yet in the leafy, moneyed suburbs of Louisville, on Park Avenue in New York or the Gold Coast of Chicago, in pricey neighborhoods in Silicon Valley or the country club districts of Kansas City or Miami, they remain an invisible part of our population, these fellow citizens who have paid such a high price.

In a nation of democratic ideals, including justice for all, this is manifestly unjust.

It is time to renew the ideal of public service for all on a national scale—and answer the call John F. Kennedy made so memorably a half century ago.

CHAPTER 10

The United States Academy of Public Service

FACT: In 2005, Teach for America had 2,181 volunteers teaching in some of the nation's most distressed school districts. By 2010 that number had more than doubled to 4,458.

According to VolunteeringinAmerica.gov, a website of the Corporation for National and Community Service, in 2010 almost seventy million Americans volunteered in a variety of public service programs. Among the states, Utah, with its strong Mormon tradition of community service, led the way: 43.5 percent of the Utah population volunteered in some fashion.

QUESTION: If the political and military establishment has no interest in a renewal of military conscription, preferring instead the current all-volunteer concept, should we have as a national priority another form of universal public service?

THE PAST

For those who choose not to go into uniform, the menu of other public service options is uneven. The Peace Corps is still a viable government agency; more than seventeen thousand applied during the economic downturn. More than eight thousand are on duty or in training for duty in seventy-seven countries, the highest totals since 2009. Since the Peace Corps was established in 1961, more than two hundred thousand have served. Even so, the Corps seems ready for a hit on the refresh button.

For my generation of males, the draft card issued when you were eighteen was a silent reminder that you owed your country military service. Every young man calculated his future by allowing for the strong possibility he would be in uniform at some point. That all came undone with Vietnam and the deeply divisive debate over just and unjust wars, college deferments, and other escape hatches. The draft went away in a storm of political and military rancor, and it is highly unlikely ever to return.

It was, at best, an uneven distribution of national obligations. Women were not eligible for the draft, and the educated and elite had more advantageous options. It is remembered now more for its liabilities than for its call to public service.

THE PRESENT

At the State Department, Secretary Hillary Clinton initiated a number of programs to expand the presence of civilian agencies in parts of the world where too much of the burden falls to the military services. In her first two years in office, working with Defense Secretary Robert Gates, she doubled the development staff of the U.S. Agency for International Development (USAID), and made several internal changes to the agency to make it more efficient and more effective.

Writing in **Foreign Affairs** magazine, she made a strong case for so-called soft power—civilian efforts in finance, construction, health services, and agriculture—describing how the United States must draw on the pool of talent that already exists within the government to build a global civilian presence with the same capability and flexibility as the military.

Clinton described the presence of civilian agencies and their highly trained employees on the ground in Iraq as "force multipliers," as they work with local groups to take responsibility for the civilian services that were decimated first by Saddam Hussein and then by war.

To those who question the expenditures on soft power and foreign economic development, especially during difficult economic times at home, Secretary Clinton argued that the investments in fact help the United States, because they strengthen fragile, failing states and create capable partners. She acknowledges not all efforts are successful in states such as Yemen and Somalia, but the alternatives are wars without end.

One of her strongest allies in this effort was the late Richard Holbrooke, a supremely gifted public servant who died too young, at the age of sixty-nine, of traumatic heart disease in late 2010. Holbrooke had been involved in American foreign policy in one form or another since his days as a junior foreign service officer in Vietnam in the sixties.

He was brilliant, brash, tireless, and unrelenting in his physical and intellectual quest to make this a better, more peaceful world. Holbrooke's appetite for difficult problems on the world stage was legendary. As a private citizen he was among the first to recognize the moral and political imperative of dealing with Africa's AIDS crisis. He was a forceful advocate for nongovernmental organizations— NGOs—that fostered greater understanding of Asia or worked on refugee problems.

When he died he was commanding a vastly expanded force of economic, agricultural, and civilian political advisers in Pakistan and Afghanistan, the most difficult assignment of his long and distinguished career. We talked often about the need to reorder the "hearts and minds" equation of America's foreign policy investments.

Personally, I think it is time to take the concept of civilian power one step further to complement the work Secretary Clinton has initiated with a major commitment to a new form of public service. Mandatory public service may be a hard political sell, but I think that bold new initiatives are in order. At the U.S. Naval Academy I outlined some thoughts for the brigade of midshipmen and an audience of academy graduates and friends.

I reminded that audience that military units in Iraq and Afghanistan have the dual and, I think, incompatible assignments of fighting the bad guys in dangerous neighborhoods and then trying to win the hearts and minds of those not shooting back. Iraqi and Afghan locals are understandably wary of heavily armed American forces who come into their villages, establish checkpoints to search for weapons, don't speak the language, and then, through an interpreter, say, "We're here to help."

During reporting trips to the region, I was embedded with military units on the front lines. An hour's helicopter ride north of Kandahar I accompanied American special forces troops into a poor village in the middle of a broad, barren valley where the Taliban had been very active. The Americans were accompanied by Afghan officers trying to raise and train a local force, and they were attempting to sell the concept to the skeptical merchants and village elders while the women looked on at a distance from behind their veils.

I asked one storekeeper whether he would welcome an Afghan force in his community. He looked around at the heavily armed Americans in their helmets, Kevlar vests, and sunglasses and said, "We don't need more people with guns telling us what to do."

I was reminded of what a former CIA terrorism expert once told me. "The problem with the Afghans," he said, "is that they have reversible turbans; their loyalty depends on who is in town." Two thousand years of foreign invaders have left them with an understandable wariness of the "we're here to help" gesture.

As for getting assistance from the locals, one encounter in an east central Afghan village at once defined the limits of their hospitality and offered a welcome laugh in the dusty intersection where members of the Tenth Mountain Division were walking that fine line between vigilance and cordiality. A gregarious Afghan man came running up to me, reached down into his raggedy robes, and produced a piece of paper worn from many folds.

He handed it to me with great pride. I opened and it read, "This is Mahmoud. He worked for me for a couple of weeks. He was just okay in his job but whatever you do, don't trust him around your personal belongings." It was signed by a U.S. Army captain. Members of the Tenth Mountain squad and I suppressed our laughs and I returned the note, saying, "You should be very proud."

Who's to blame the Afghans for taking whatever advantage they can, after all they have been through in their long history of one occupational force after another—all men with guns telling them what to do?

It's not the fault of the highly trained and well-meaning American forces. They just have incompatible missions and not enough of the right kind of help for the hearts and minds equation. For example, when the U.S. military units set up medical offices in rural areas, they were generally staffed by male combatants, which meant Muslim fathers wouldn't send their daughters there for examinations or treatments.

THE PROMISE

I returned from two Afghan trips wondering, Couldn't we establish a Peace Corps Plus or a Diplomatic Special Forces? Highly trained adventurous young Americans who take up the hearts and minds mission? These would be noncombatants stationed in forward operating bases as physicians, educators, technicians, agriculture experts, and engineers.

USAID has committed and capable staff members doing this kind of work in the world, but as effective and passionate as they are, USAID workers have almost no public profile at home to draw in this country's best and brightest.

In this age of portable technology, why couldn't instructional programs in midwifery, fundamental health practices, basic hygiene, water projects, nutrition, or agriculture be downloaded and fed through portable satellite dishes powered by portable, gas-fueled generators in modular structures placed in the village center? A small team of Peace Corps Plus technicians could set up such an arrangement in a short time and the U.S. government could launch a satellite dedicated to making just these kinds of programs available around the world, in an electronic glossary of languages.

The twenty-first century should be a time for new, big, and bold ideas for a renewed America. It is time to establish public service institutions that are as prestigious and successful as the military academies so that people who are dedicated to their country but unable or unwilling to serve in the armed forces have a complementary opportunity.

Why not develop a group of public service academies attached to land grant colleges and universities in a half dozen or so geographic regions? The intensive courses in languages, education, health, construction, and conflict resolution could range from twelve months to two years. When I discussed this in the presence of Bob McNair, a self-made entrepreneur who owns the Houston Texans of the National Football League, he had a good idea: Make the academies a public-private partnership.

Imagine, say, a Johnson & Johnson fellowship in Third World medicine, at a state university. Or a Caterpillar fellowship in road construction; a GE fellowship in power generators or clean-water systems; an AT&T fellowship in telecommunications; a Bill and Melinda Gates Foundation fellowship in health systems. Corporate America would be helping to train people, who could then operate outside the United States, or inside.

The win-win for corporate America, which is increasingly operating outside the borders of the United States, is that the public service fellows would get accelerated training in can-do management skills that they could put to work abroad and then bring to the home office once their fellowship ends.

Academy enrollees would be paid a subsistence wage during their training and then compensated at military levels once they graduate. As an incentive, their income would be tax free for three years, which could be the minimum commitment for every volunteer.

Paul Farmer, the American physician who has dedicated his life to establishing clinics and bringing First World health care to Third World countries such as Rwanda and Haiti, should be a consultant in the construction and content of the curriculum and the training necessary to turn out productive graduates.

David Harris, who first came to America's attention during the antiwar movement of the sixties, is now a journalist, author, and a baby boomer who can look back on a life lived honorably. He was Stanford University's student body president and a leading voice against the Vietnam War in 1968.

Instead of burning his draft card or running off to Canada, he simply refused the call of the Selective Service System and went to federal prison for twenty months. He now lives in a log home in a eucalyptus grove high in Marin County, north of San Francisco. His inner flame continues to burn.

I interviewed Harris for a taping about the legacy of the baby boomers. "The body politic has to step away from its own militarization and understand we're gonna survive in the future by our capacity to make common cause with as many other people as we can," he said. "The big issues facing us are the ones that demand a kind of global unanimity if we have any hope of survival. Climate change and health issues are not going to be solved by armies. As long as we relate to the rest of the world just through militaries, we're not gonna be able to grapple with the issues that are really gonna kill us."

The assignments of these daring new young men and women in soft power public service would not be confined to operations in war zones.

We now live on a crowded planet where natural disasters have cataclysmic consequences. The 2004 tsunami, the 2005 Kashmir earthquake, Katrina, the 2010 Haiti earthquake: All drew the U.S. military as first responders.

Matt Pottinger, the son of a longtime friend, was a **Wall Street Journal** reporter based in China when the killer tsunami struck Southeast Asia in 2004. He rushed to cover it and came away so impressed with the esprit de corps and quality of the U.S. Marines he met, it changed his life.

He went back to Beijing, befriended Marines stationed at the U.S. embassy, and persuaded them to help him to train as an officer candidate for their service. It was not easy—he was thirty-two at the time—but he made it and served with distinction on two deployments to Afghanistan and one in Iraq before returning to the United States to become a Fellow at the Council on Foreign Relations in New York.

"I have zero regrets about my decision," he told me, adding, "Becoming a Marine opened my eyes to aspects of my country I would not have understood if I had stayed a journalist."

As a primary example, he cites the role of the military as an integrator of social and ethnic groups in which everyone has an equal opportunity and there are common expectations and standards.

"Take the Marine Corps," he said. "It depends on excellence at the bottom and so those at the top are responsible for training and molding the grunts. If an officer doesn't get that job done, he's held accountable.

"As a result," he said, "I go out on patrol with a Marine squad in Iraq and the leader is a twenty-year-old corporal who is part sociologist, part waterworks engineer and full-time warrior. He has awesome responsibility.

"Why can't the Marine Corps model be an example for education reform?"

Pottinger is troubled by one critical missing element in the military ranks. "We have the middle class and the working class, we have a representative ethnic mix but we don't have the elites. That's wrong."

As a result, when it comes to decision making in Washington, where the elites dominate the salons of power, Pottinger notes that "more mistakes are made by non-vets than veterans when it comes to military matters."

For this son of privilege, with his Chinese-language skills and degree from the University of Massachusetts, the bottom line is this: "I understand my country better from inside a military uniform than I did as a civilian and as a journalist."

Nonetheless, he also fully understands we're rooted by law, custom, and experience in a civilian society.

To my mind, we ask too much of the military and not enough of the rest of us when it comes to putting forward our greatest strengths.

Soldiers, guardsmen, and Marines bring discipline, energy, and authority to their assignments, but in a world in which the U.S. military is already stretched thin to fulfill its combat missions, it should be a national priority to develop a civilian force to meet the needs of domestic and international disasters.

Our daughter Jennifer, a seasoned emergency room physician who spent six months working with refugees on the Pakistan-Afghan border, volunteered for duty at the time of Katrina and came away frustrated with the inefficiencies of the organization thrown together to meet the needs of displaced residents of New Orleans. When she arrived at the Memphis airport there was not a one-stop desk for physicians to check in, present their credentials—which could be certified online—and report to the area of their expertise.

She spent most of her exasperating first day trying to get credentials and an assignment so she could put her physician's skills to work. In the future, wouldn't it make sense if she were to carry a card certifying her ER credentials so when she reported to a disaster zone the card could be fed into a computer at a single site and she could be assigned a task within moments?

In this increasingly crowded world, natural and manmade disasters will have ever larger consequences and will require a first response that is cohesive, efficient, and interdependent. Hurricanes and exploding oil wells along the U.S. Gulf Coast, tornadoes and floods in the heartland, and homegrown terrorist attacks such as the bombing of the Alfred P. Murrah Federal Building in Oklahoma City are all the domestic equivalents of war, assaulting the general welfare of the citizens affected, disrupting commerce and education, and destroying property values.

A new army of public service cadets could be a huge asset for federal, local, and international agencies responsible for managing the crises.

There is a long and rich national history of Americans finding common cause and responding with a common effort. Let us not forget that the Founding Fathers represented many beliefs but were bound together by a determination to establish free will as a governing principle.

The pioneers of the nineteenth century who pushed oxen teams and rode horses into the Great Plains and Rocky Mountain West were from different origins and brought with them different faiths but also a singular determination to expand their new country's horizon and give it a latticework of community, economic development, and political opportunity. The organized labor movement of the early and mid-twentieth century was a courageous populist uprising against the rapacious exploitation of workers by wealthy interests who answered primarily to their own greed. The civil rights movement of the sixties forced a moral and legal resolution of racism by uniting like-minded citizens of many colors and standings.

We are witness to America's great common heart whenever there is a natural disaster, and not just in our country. Haiti could not have coped without the instant response of humanitarians from around the world, most of them from the United States. It was not just a weekend commitment. Thousands of people from a wide range of organizations encamped for weeks at a time under difficult conditions.

Our youngest daughter, Sarah, a trained therapist, spent three weeks living in a tent and dodging rodents as she tended to the needs of abused and abandoned women as a grief counselor. Another group of American volunteers parachuted into an isolated mountaintop Haitian village to provide emergency food and medical relief before they cleared a landing strip for a more efficient resupply procedure.

Whenever disaster strikes at home or anywhere in the world American relief workers are always among the first to arrive and last to leave. Volunteering is part of our American character, born from the hard work of creating a democratic republic when none existed elsewhere and then taming a wild and majestic land.

We take the measure of our fellow citizens by their willingness to step beyond their own needs to help others. Every community has service clubs, veterans organizations, church groups, affiliates of national relief organizations, and homegrown charitable enterprises infused with the understanding that we all owe something beyond our personal needs.

For an emerging generation of Americans, now is an opportunity to renew and strengthen that tradition of rising to meet the challenges an unpredictable world places in its path.

CHAPTER 11

Stepping Up and
Signing Up

FACT: There is no shortage of opportunities to volunteer and have an impact. United Way, the umbrella organization for community groups, launched a recruiting drive in the spring of 2011 to find one million volunteers to read, tutor, and mentor in inner-city schools. A website called Service Nation is a gathering place for individuals and organizations that are concentrating on using their talents to restart the American Dream following the Great Recession.

QUESTION: If John F. Kennedy were around today and asked what you'd done for your country recently, how would you answer?

A public-private partnership to institutionalize public service would be an ambitious project requiring a formidable amount of cooperation, coordination, and cash to launch but it would have at the ready an essential element: the volunteer spirit within the American character.

It has long been part of the national ethos to step forward when the need is obvious but unresolved. In my lifetime I have been witness to large and small enterprises organized to great effect by selfless citizens with no motive other than to give voice and support to a cause that will benefit all of society.

THE PAST

It was not that long ago that Los Angeles residents thought smog was just a price to be paid for progress. When we first moved to Southern California in the summer of 1966, the city was enveloped daily in a yellow acrid cloud. Later that year the cooling winds of fall came through and the smog lifted. Meredith got up one morning and was startled to see a mountain range in the distance out our window. For several months it had been completely obscured by the smoggy haze. She had had no idea it existed.

It was plainly obvious that the smog was an acute health hazard and a drag on the region's economic future—who wants to live in an emphysema zone?

Clean air standards were eventually introduced, including rigid new requirements for automobile and industrial emissions. Automobiles now burn 60 percent less gasoline than they did in 1972. Slowly, the mountains surrounding the San Fernando Valley began to be seen with more regularity.

Across the country, young people weaned on activism and drawn to nature were giving new muscle to organizations such as the Sierra Club, the Environmental Defense Fund, Conservation International, the Nature Conservancy, and thousands of local organizations dedicated to slowing or stopping altogether the degradation of natural resources.

President Richard Nixon established the Environmental Protection Agency, the EPA, to set national standards for land, water, and air use for the greater good, recognizing the fundamental fact of nature: It is all-encompassing. State lines and private property boundaries are no barriers to polluted air, contaminated water, or ecosystem destruction. Recent efforts by conservative forces in Congress to either eliminate or greatly weaken the EPA are bewildering to anyone who lived with the unchecked hazards of dirty air, polluted water, and degraded land not so long ago.

The environmental movement was a classic example of a populist-driven change in American life, but we have miles to go before we arrive at a sensible place. Here's a question I invariably ask myself as I drive along Interstate 405, the multilane stretch of highway connecting the most populated areas of Southern California.

The diamond carpool lanes, where only vehicles with two or more passengers are allowed, are invariably free of congestion while the other lanes are bumper-to-bumper with single-passenger cars and trucks, burning oil-based fuel at a ferocious rate. I'm often one of them, the lone passenger in a high-powered rental car, going to or returning from a visit with my mother in Orange County.

What, I wonder, would my fellow travelers say if we could somehow poll them right now about the absurdity of what we're all doing, encasing ourselves one by one in these expensive and muscular vehicles with rapacious appetites?

I then try to imagine a future economist or historian, say a century from now, looking back on this scene and trying to understand how we failed to act on the obvious need to urgently develop alternative forms of transportation when the evidence of the political, economic, and environmental perils of carbon-based energy were so overwhelming. Will our freeways become our Easter Island giant statues? Only the pavement will remain.

We seem to be, at best, reluctantly lurching toward more mass transit and alternative energy vehicles. I am personally persuaded that the most effective approach to the scientifically indisputable fact of climate change and the consequences for Mother Earth will be generational. Young people coming of age now are not conditioned by past practices and head-in-the-sand attitudes about what's possible. They will lead the way in determining new sources of energy and more efficient transportation systems and utilities, in conservation of resources, and in adjusting lifestyles for sustainability.

THE PRESENT

Where is the popular uprising that has been so effective in other areas? There are no two better examples than MADD, Mothers Against Drunk Driving, and Susan G. Komen for the Cure, the national crusade to find a cure for breast cancer.

MADD was started by Candace Lightner in 1980 when her thirteen-year-old daughter was struck and killed by a drunken driver. Before Lightner began publicizing the heartbreaking stories of families who had lost a member to drunken drivers, the mix of alcohol and the highway was a fixture in American life. Laws on the books were enforced unevenly, and there was no designated driver concept in the culture.

The resulting carnage and grief was overshadowed by the myth that weaving your way home from a party was part of the macho entitlement of getting a driver's license. I shudder when I remember my own youthful behavior behind the wheel or as a passenger when too much booze had been consumed.

MADD changed all that. More than thirty years later, drunken-driving fatalities have been cut in half, the national drinking age has been raised to twenty-one, and law enforcement agencies have instituted a policy of zero tolerance when it comes to driving while intoxicated. One angry, grief-stricken mother started it all and made our highways a much safer place.

In the fall of 2010, I was invited by a longtime friend, Celia Miner, to return to South Dakota and help draw attention to Susan G. Komen for the Cure. It was started by Nancy Brinker as a pledge to her sister, Susan Komen, as she was dying of breast cancer.

Nancy, a tall, striking brunette, had learned marketing skills working at Neiman Marcus and had a wide network of friends so, as she says, "With two hundred dollars and a shoe box full of names to call for help" she started a phenomenal consciousness-raising campaign.

My friend Celia is a breast cancer survivor, and

Celia Miner, a breast cancer survivor
and Komen activist

it seemed like showing up for a Saturday morning registration of a Race for the Cure event was the least I could do. I was not prepared for the turnout—more than four thousand runners registered at the University of South Dakota—or for the passion of the cancer survivors with whom I had lunch.

They were businesswomen, stay-at-home moms, teachers, and lawyers. One was a clinical biologist working on breast cancer issues. It was a cheerful, upbeat gathering, and any stranger looking on might have thought it was a sorority reunion with the campus so close at hand. This sisterhood, however, was bound by the ordeal of breast cancer and the welcome fact of survival.

This was shortly before the 2010 midterm elections and political rhetoric was reaching incendiary levels, but in the Komen group I couldn't tell a conservative from a liberal. They were united by their common condition and courage and more than eager to spread the message about the importance of regular checkups and the need to raise money for research and various treatments.

My personal radar about the Komen organization turned to high and in the following days and weeks I was astonished by the pink presence of Komen organizers everywhere, including at NFL football games. During October, National Breast Cancer Awareness Month, some of the largest, toughest athletes in the world played their hard-hitting games while wearing pink shoelaces or chin-straps as a reminder of the cause.

Komen affiliates have raised more than $1 billion since 1982 for education, screening, and treatment programs, especially for women who otherwise might not be able to afford what they need. Cancer specialists credit Komen for the Cure as a major factor in the statistic that matters most: There are now two and a half million breast cancer survivors, more than any other cancer group.

Nancy Brinker's pledge to her dying sister to raise the consciousness of the nation regarding breast cancer has been realized in the form of a powerful global organization with affiliates in 120 U.S. communities and more than one hundred thousand survivors and activists signed up for the cause. The pyramids in Egypt, the Empire State Building in New York, and the White House have all been "pinked" as a reminder of the work remaining.

While she was doing this, Brinker also served as chief of protocol and the U.S. ambassador to Hungary during the George W. Bush administration. She is now devoted full-time to Komen for the Cure, living and working in Washington, D.C.

Komen is not universally popular in the field. Some breast cancer survivors and organizations have complained it is too protective of its trademarked phrase "for the cure" and that it spends too much money on big stunts.

Neither MADD nor Komen is perfect, but they have made profoundly important contributions to society and they grew from the ground up, not the top down. They share another characteristic: They were started by members of the baby boom, a generation who grew up believing they could change the world, and when they were given the opportunity they did not hesitate.

Wealthy baby boomers are taking that can-do attitude to a new level. The aforementioned Bill and Melinda Gates Foundation is the apotheosis of a new generation taking a hands-on and concomitant financial commitment to help those who need it most. The Gates' personal and financial effort is so ambitious and so far reaching in developing relief or cures for some of the most vexing medical problems in remote corners of the world it will surely be remembered as one of the most impressive developments of the twenty-first century.

They are redefining philanthropy even more impressively than Andrew Carnegie and Henry Ford did before them. Their joint and very impressive effort with Warren Buffett to enlist other billionaires in a campaign to give away half their wealth before they die is another breakthrough that will find a prominent place in any history of great wealth and how it was managed.

They were following the earlier suggestion of their fellow billionaire Ted Turner, who in the mid-nineties committed $1 billion to the United Nations and said to anyone who would listen, "We don't need another Forbes Five Hundred list of the wealthiest people in the world; we need a Forbes Five Hundred List of those who give away the most money." Gates and Buffett are at the top of that list, and they are on a global mission to ask others to join them.

Buffett's generosity has not diminished his self-mocking penurious ways. When I once remarked to him about Bill Gates's hair, which looked as if it had been styled by a pruning shear, Warren laughed, referred to his own rumpled appearance, and said, "I often tell people Bill and I are so rich because we share a comb."

A comb, vast fortunes, and a determination to leave the world a better place without seeking recognition in the form of piles of brick with their names attached.

They're not alone.

For all of the criticism directed at Wall Street during the Great Recession, a good deal of it justly deserved, it did not deter what is arguably America's greatest urban all-volunteer good-deed organization. It is called the Robin Hood Foundation and it was the brainchild of Paul Tudor Jones, a Memphis native and University of Virginia graduate who came to New York determined to strike it rich or go dead broke trying.

Fortunately for the five boroughs of New York, rich won out: He became fabulously wealthy as one of the pioneers of the hedge fund movement. By the time he was in his midthirties Jones was already a member of the B class, as in "billionaire."

No one enjoyed his newfound money more. An avid sportsman, he built shooting and fishing lodges in upstate New York, the Chesapeake Bay, the Florida Keys, Colorado, Africa, and Argentina. Then he had a bold idea for his hedge fund colleagues that went well beyond their personal possessions and pleasures.

Shortly after the stock market's spectacular dive in 1987, Paul summoned three other venture capitalists—Glenn Dubin, Maurice Chessa, and Peter Borish—to his Manhattan bachelor pad for takeout Chinese food and a big idea: We have to take care of our neighbors who are not as fortunate. Also attending was David Saltzman, who has been Robin Hood's peerless executive director ever since.

Jones enlisted them in an idealistic crusade to eliminate poverty in New York. Not just reduce it. Eliminate it. That was their goal and they set out to do it in a businesslike manner.

They assembled a first-rate professional staff and settled on four goals: education, early childhood development, job training, and shelter. Once the Robin Hood Foundation was up and running, already established social agencies could apply for funds, but the standard was high. The board, which financed all the headquarters expenses so every other dime hit the streets, took a corporate approach to their philanthropy. Robin Hood staffers appraised the central mission of each prospective agency, pored over its books, sized up the personnel, and then established goals—metrics—for the agency to meet or the funding would be cut off.

When I first encountered Robin Hood at a congratulatory breakfast it organized every year to celebrate the accomplishments of their clients, I was deeply skeptical, even though many of the board members were friends. Rich guys, I thought, trying to buy some respectability. I was half right. Most of them were rich—very rich—but they were also altruistic.

In almost twenty-five years Robin Hood has raised and spent $1.25 billion in New York City, winning the support of Democrats and Republicans alike. They've built charter schools and housed homeless veterans, funded shelters for abused children and unwed mothers, and established work-training programs and food banks.

At Robin Hood's annual breakfast, titans of Wall Street, society matrons, and celebrity athletes such as Eli Manning and Lance Armstrong are moved to tears as they listen to former junkies, homeless moms, and abused kids bear witness in emotional narratives to the help they've gotten from Robin Hood–supported agencies, never failing with their message to remind the wealthy breakfast guests of the real value of their dollars.

At an annual gala, which sometimes tilts over to the excessive side, the Jacob K. Javits Convention Center in New York is converted into the prom everyone wants to attend. The entertainers have included Jon Stewart, Lady Gaga, Aretha Franklin, Aerosmith, the Black Eyed Peas, the late Ray Charles, Stevie Wonder, Beyoncé and Jay-Z, John Mellencamp, Robin Williams, and Whoopi Goldberg.

The young, rich crowd bids astronomical amounts for prizes such as a walk-on part in a Gwyneth Paltrow movie or a seat at the Oscars. A VIP trip to the Beijing Olympics went for more than $2 million. Tom Brady of the New England Patriots auctioned off a visit to his training camp for more than $500,000.

In 2009, financial wizard and philanthropist George Soros announced he would put up $50 million in a Robin Hood matching grant challenge, and the Robin Hood crowd met the challenge. Eighty million dollars was raised in a single night.

It all went to schools, job-training programs, housing for the homeless, and food banks.

Robin Hood didn't blink when the Great Recession hit, raising a record amount at its annual galas in 2009 and 2010. Jon Stewart set the tone for the evening in 2009 when he said, "You're going to donate a lot of money tonight; not enough, however, to offset all the s—t you've done." It got a big laugh and an even bigger response at the bottom line.

No other city in America has access to as much private wealth as greater New York, but this is about more than the money. It's about the idea and the selfless execution. Robin Hood could be a template for other cities on a smaller scale.

So could the mission of a former Rhodes scholar turned Navy SEAL.

Eric Greitens isn't waiting for a public service academy to turn out a new generation of public servants. He's establishing his own corps from the growing ranks of wounded veterans of Iraq and Afghanistan. He calls it "The Mission Continues," a phrase that came to mind during a visit to the National Naval Medical Center in Bethesda.

Lieutenant Greitens, a Navy SEAL who served in Iraq and Afghanistan, was recovering from his own combat wounds, which were not extensive, when he went to check on some of his more seriously injured comrades. Making conversation, he asked what they wanted to do when they recovered. To a man, they said they wanted to return to their units. One young man summed up the spirit of the ward: "I lost my legs," he said. "That's all. I did not lose my desire to serve or my pride in being an American."

The powerful idea of continuing service even after paying such a high price led Greitens and his friend Kenneth Harbaugh to form The Mission Continues, a 501(c)(3) that places wounded vets in fourteen-week fellowship programs with charitable organizations such as the Boys and Girls Clubs of America. They get cost-of-living expenses and a renewed sense of worth. The organizations get a well-trained and highly motivated volunteer.

When I met Eric at a VA hospital in St. Louis I thought, Here's a modest young man with nothing to be modest about. He was an honors student at Duke University before earning a PhD in political science at Oxford University as a Rhodes scholar. His doctoral thesis was called "Children First," a study he conducted to determine the most effective ways humanitarian organizations can help children affected by war.

Eric's work in places such as Rwanda, the Gaza

Eric Greitens, founder of
The Mission Continues

Strip, Croatia, and Albania resulted in an award-winning collection of his photographs in the report **Save the Children: Community Strategies for Healing,** a publication of the Save the Children Foundation, Zimbabwe University, and Duke University.

After Oxford, he could have opted for the cushy, tweedy life of a college professor but instead he volunteered for the Navy SEALS, the elite warriors who earn their place by undergoing a six-week training program that pushes the candidates to the very edge of physical, psychological, and emotional surrender.

Following his combat tours in Afghanistan and Iraq, Eric returned home to earn one of the highly competitive slots as a White House fellow, the prestigious program that boasts Colin Powell, Kansas governor Sam Brownback, former labor secretary Elaine Chao, and retired CNN chief executive Tom Johnson among its graduates.

As he moved back into civilian life, Eric never forgot the first and last rule of military leadership. As he told me in our first meeting, "You take care of your guys and just because we came off the battlefield, that doesn't mean we're gonna stop taking care of them."

We were in a rehabilitation ward for severe spinal cord injuries, watching Jamey Bollinger, an Army veteran who was caught in an IED detonation in Iraq, patiently go through his therapy routine, his lifeless legs and arms hooked up to electronic stimulators and motors so he could exercise in hopes of regaining some muscle tone. Jamey, from a small town just across the state line in Illinois, was dressed in a St. Louis Cardinals jersey and baseball cap and much more eager to talk about the Redbirds' pennant chances than his injuries.

"Jamey's a perfect example," Eric said. "We have so many wounded and disabled veterans coming back in their twenties and we want to be sure we're there for them fifty, sixty, seventy years from now. Their whole community needs to be around them, not just for the first six months but for the rest of their lives."

The best way to do that, Eric believes, is to find a role for the wounded vets in their communities, to give them an opportunity to serve so they're not just dependent on someone else. In the long wars in Iraq and Afghanistan, an estimated thirty thousand Americans have been wounded in combat or seriously injured in war-zone accidents.

In many cases, the wounds are so severe the injured would not have lived just twenty years ago, but thanks to greatly enhanced on-site treatment, speedy evacuation, and especially the advanced surgical and medical procedures once the wounded reach a base hospital, the survival rate is by far the best of any war in which the United States has been involved.

That's unconditionally good news, but it also means those with severely debilitating conditions—paralysis, blindness, brain injuries—will require special assistance the rest of their lives. "The Pentagon and Veterans' Administration have to find better models for reintroducing the vets into society," Eric said. "The VA still is a hospital model—for treatment and release. Local communities, many of them small towns in the rural areas, have to take ownership of their native sons and daughters returning with lifelong wounds and limited futures. We've got to figure out a way to help those communities. The government can pay but that's just a start."

THE PROMISE

By mid-2010 he had sixty-six full-time fellows, and more than four hundred vets had gone through the program. One of them, Phillip Sturgeon, a fourteen-year Army veteran, suffered head injuries and had developed post-traumatic stress disorder when I met him at the VA hospital in St. Louis. He was training a Labrador pup to be a service dog for the

physically challenged. He called the dog L.T., short
for "Lieutenant."

Before Sturgeon heard about The Mission Continues, he had about given up, and it was a strain
on his family. "I thought my service and I thought
my life was pretty much at an end," Sturgeon told
me as we sat on a gurney in the hospital's spinal
cord rehabilitation ward while Jamey Bollinger
continued his workout at the other end, assisted by
a team of cheerful, athletic young women specially
trained for this kind of therapy.

Sturgeon, a large, quiet man—shy, really, except
when he lights up about L.T.—went on, "L.T. gives
me purpose. He helps me deal with anxiety every
day and he gives me purpose because I know by
training him I'm giving back to the community.
When I finish with his training he can help someone in a wheelchair."

Sturgeon hopes The Mission Continues will also
help educate the civilian population about the
debilitating effects of PTSD. "I don't think a lot of
people understand how it affects the guys who
come home, their families, how they live through
the nightmares and sleepless nights. Not knowing
how to adjust to everyday life after being in a situ-
ation like that [Iraq] every day."

As L.T. pulled on his leash and Sturgeon's wife
and a daughter listened in, smiling, Sturgeon said,

Phillip Sturgeon, wounded
in Iraq and now a part of
The Mission Continues

nodding to the puppy, "That gives me something to look forward to and it was a huge relief because it brought my whole family back together."

Phillip Sturgeon's whole family includes his father, a Vietnam veteran, confined to a wheelchair because of wounds he suffered in that war. When Sturgeon finished his training, L.T. became the service dog for his father.

As I was writing this in Montana after a beautiful, sunny day of fly-fishing and horseback riding with my family, Greitens sent an update on Sturgeon that rocked me emotionally. He wrote that as a result of his traumatic brain injury, "Phil is losing his vision and will soon be blind. Since his original plan to train service dogs is no longer possible we've found a place for him with the Red Cross."

My God, I thought, how much does one family have to go through? How many Phil Sturgeons are out there, in small towns, second- or third-generation military vets so disabled?

We must ensure they are not consigned to a life of constant difficulties, surrounded by the indifference of their fellow citizens.

PART THREE

Help Me Make It Through This New Dot-Com Age

CHAPTER 12

Wire the World but Don't Short-Circuit Your Soul

> **FACT:** More than a billion people a day sign on to the Internet for commerce, communication, or research on everything from junior high term papers to complex and sophisticated medical, academic, economic, and political issues; they're looking for a mate or a used book, a new weapons system or an ant farm. There has never been such a transformative technology so instantly and easily available.
>
> **QUESTION:** When was the last time you had a conversation in school, at work, or in a bar about the real meaning of all this communication capacity? Or, as a Stanford law student said to me, "When are we going to have a serious discussion about the new meaning of 'friend'?"

For some reason I am still invited to deliver college commencement speeches, a flattering but demanding exercise because I use the occasions to take the measure of what I think I've learned in the past four years and what may be useful to graduates one-third my age.

In the week preceding my 2006 commencement address at Stanford, the student newspaper interviewed graduating seniors, asking what they thought of me as a choice to launch them on their way. One young woman said, "Tom Brokaw? That's like listening to adult radio."

So when I took the podium I singled her out by name and said, "Turn your iPod to adult radio if you'd like, but I have something to say to your classmates that may have more relevance."

It got a big laugh, and her parents caught up to me later to say, in effect, "She had it coming."

What I tried to do that day for those students in the heart of Silicon Valley, at the womb of so many cyberspace geniuses, is to remind them of a wider obligation that goes well beyond logging on.

They are the pioneers of a technology that is changing our lives and our world at such a pace that it can outrun judgment. Information technology, the cosmos of the Internet hooked up to laptops and desktops, smartphones and digital cameras, Facebook, Twitter, and YouTube, satellite and cable television, and who knows what someone in a garage in Silicon Valley is working on next.

Cornelius Vanderbilt, J. P. Morgan, Henry Ford, John D. Rockefeller, and the other men who built the American industrial and financial foundation in the nineteenth and twentieth centuries are fixed parts of the national memory for their boldness, wealth, willful manners, and larger-than-life personal lifestyles.

Future generations will be studying the likes of Bill Gates of Microsoft, Steve Jobs of Apple, Sergey Brin and Larry Page of Google, Mark Zuckerberg of Facebook, and who knows what other cyber pioneers with the same fascination my generation had for the earlier titans.

This new universe they've created with other cyber-geniuses around the world has an infinite capacity for constant expansion, but we do know that in its seminal stage it is already profoundly changing communication, commerce, research, medicine, and social structure everywhere.

The physical properties of this transformative epoch are self-evident. What gets too little attention are the limits, a subject I try to encourage younger generations to engage.

You cannot eliminate poverty or disease by hitting the delete key.

You cannot reverse global warming by striking backspace.

Nuclear proliferation, political and religious

imperialism, and natural disasters won't disappear when you hit delete. (Control-alt-delete is also how you access the home page.)

It will do us little good to wire the world if we short-circuit our souls.

The hard work of constantly improving life on this precious planet requires people willing to put their boots on the ground, get their hands dirty, and spend their nights in scary places.

No text message will ever replace the first kiss. "I luv u" on a tiny screen will never replace that declaration whispered into your ear at the end of a long embrace. Holding a BlackBerry cannot compare with holding hands on a first date or exchanging spoken vows on a wedding day. I never want to hear a lyric that goes, "A tweet is just a tweet—as time goes by."

If I am asked to give a wedding toast, I remind the couple that no GPS system or Google map will show them the way to a long, happy union. In fact, the electronic guides can lull their users into a kind of lethargy that does not serve them well when the batteries run low or the devices are misplaced.

It's a much wider world than the small screen on your laptop, smartphone, or GPS device. I know those devices can be helpful, but I will never forget my first encounter with their use. I was emerging from a backcountry fishing trip in the wilderness area north of Yellowstone when I encountered a small party of day hikers running around frantically just off the trail. When I asked if there was something wrong, one of them explained they were with a Stanford professor who was testing one of the new handheld GPS devices.

During a break he'd set it down and then resumed his hike, inadvertently leaving it behind. They were desperately trying to find it. I laughed to myself as I thought of the device lying on a bed of pine needles, knowing exactly where it was, while the hapless hikers acted like a small herd of sheep untethered from their herder.

THE PAST

To offer some historic perspective, think of the beginning of the twentieth century, when other forms of new technologies were sweeping the developed world: electricity, telephones, airplanes, automobiles, breakthroughs in medicine. It was the beginning of the American Century, and the possibilities were endless.

Before the hundred years ended, we had been involved in two world wars, endured a crushing Great Depression, and witnessed holocausts in Europe, Africa, and Southeast Asia. Russia became the Soviet Union, a cruel and cold-blooded oppressor of the most basic human rights, all in the name of liberating the proletariat. China, that ancient civilization of invention, culture, and philosophy, was converted into a closed landscape of thought control and commune economies better suited to the nineteenth century than the twentieth.

THE PRESENT

It is folly to discount both the proven and still-untested transformative applications of these new technologies. In every conceivable way they are game changers. We're in a global race to keep up with their ramifications and impact in every aspect of life. What we're missing, however, is a national dialogue about the wise use of these powerful instruments of communication. In the hands of reckless or vindictive users they are used for intimidation and malice. They can be the electronic equivalent of pulling a pin on a grenade and rolling the explosive into someone's private life—what came to be called "fragging" in Vietnam.

In the fall of 2010, a Rutgers college student committed suicide after his roommate streamed video on the Internet of him having a sexual encounter with another male. Other teenagers have been driven to suicide or depression by website bullying and humiliation. The easy temptations of information technology can swiftly outrun judgment. It is not unique to America.

Imagine the task ahead for Chinese leaders as they try to manage a booming economy, a mix of state and private controls, the move of millions of people from the countryside into more settled areas, and the building of industries that will provide jobs and finance necessary infrastructure—all while remaining determined to retain political control and restrict outside influences.

The ultimate test for the leadership of China may be its attempts to control access to the Internet. The Politburo may be able to control elections, restrict free speech, direct the economy, manipulate international currency markets, determine who shall go to school where, and dispense swift, brutal punishment to those who fail to fall in line, but controlling access to the Internet? The Internet is oxygen to a new generation and there are simply too many ways to access it in this vast new universe that has been created. For all of their cunning and exceptional managerial skills in bringing China from the eighteenth century to the twenty-first in the past thirty years, for Chinese leaders to think they can wall off the Internet is the modern equivalent of their ancestors thinking the Great Wall of

China could hold back marauding nomadic tribes in the fifth century B.C.

As you read this, a clever young Chinese student is hacking his or her way through the Beijing firewall, breaking into the brave new world where the riches of information and the excitement of social networking are pulsing with possibilities.

The Chinese leadership, to say nothing of their counterparts in every corner of the globe, would be far better served if they redirected their efforts to making the Internet work for them rather than restricting its use.

When the Internet took hold in our society, a number of friends would come to me and say things like, "You can't believe little Johnny; he's an absolute whiz on his computer. He's on the keyboard late every night!" When I then asked, "Do you have any idea where Johnny the keyboard master is going with his new space-age powers?" they'd look at me with blank or slightly worried expressions. "No?" I'd say. "Well, you'd better find out."

Later they'd come to me with anguished expressions, saying, "When I approach his room I hear a quick clickety-clack of the keys and then computer snapping shut. What do I do?"

The honest answer? "Beats me."

Of course, the more responsible response is to

encourage the same kind of dialogue you'd have with a child when they reach driving age or when they begin to experiment with drugs or alcohol (and they will). Develop your own Internet computer skills so you can relate at roughly the same level. Share your favorite discoveries and ask them to share theirs with you. Explore together.

This new universe has its own rules so that not even grown-ups who work with young people every day are conscious of what's going on outside their supervision. I was amused when the very upscale school district of New Canaan, Connecticut, decided to set up an elaborate monitoring and filtering system when President Obama was scheduled to address the nation's students on the importance of studying productively and supporting one another.

On **Meet the Press** I was critical of New Canaan and other school districts who imagined something sinister in the president's motives, pointing out that for me, this was not a partisan issue. I reminded everyone that President Reagan did something similar when he was in office.

The New Canaan superintendent of schools was upset by my criticism and called to complain. He had a rather tortured explanation for the district's censorious attitude and so I finally asked, "Do your students bring their personal computers to school?"

"Yes," he replied.

Then I asked, "Do you monitor or filter what they access on their computers?"

"No," he said.

"I rest my case," I replied. He wanted to stand between his students and the president of the United States but he had not a clue what they were reading on their computers during school hours and in the presence of teachers and administrators.

Equally unsettling are schools that permit smartphones in the classroom without realizing that some students surreptitiously use them to cheat. A strategically placed phone with its browser open to Google is too easy to arrange.

As we go careening into this brave new world of on-the-go information available at a keystroke, shouldn't we have an ongoing conversation about the origins, agendas, credibility, and context of the information we're retrieving? Take, for example, the sometimes bizarre claims dropped into Wikipedia entries like errant mortar rounds.

It took me several tries to eradicate an utterly false Wikipedia statement that on the day of the 9/11 attacks I had chanted "War, war, war" on the air like a militant yell leader. A Los Angeles friend, a screaming heterosexual who depends on his secretary to guide him through cyberspace, was startled to read in his Wikipedia entry that he was the first openly gay senior partner of a major law firm.

———

Personal computers have been accurately described as the first technology in which the children are teaching the parents to drive. Parents and other grown-ups need not concede this territory to their offspring. We'd better get behind the wheel ourselves.

Older boomers and my generation, slightly older, are at the tail end of the user population, representing less than 13 percent of those going online. There are now a number of online sites dedicated to teaching seniors how to get with the Internet program. For those too intimidated by online instruction, senior citizen centers around the country are establishing in-house tutorials using local young people as instructors and counselors.

There is a bonus in all of this. Dr. Laura Carstensen of the Stanford Center on Longevity reports that one of the ways to slow the aging process is to learn entirely new skills. "It's not enough," she says, "to do crosswords or play bridge, relying on your memory bank; you should try to learn something entirely new." Director Gary Small at the UCLA Longevity Center concurs. "The new technology will create a major milestone in brain evolution," he said, explaining that Internet use among seniors dramatically increases brain activity.

It's not that baby boomers and those of us in the generation just ahead are Luddites when it comes to cyber technology and the vast new universe of the information age. During conversations with Facebook founder Mark Zuckerberg and his rock star chief operating officer Sheryl Sandberg, I've pressed them for reasons why I should at this age add one more electronic chore to my email, Google, Bing, Yahoo! list.

Sheryl immediately took me to a Facebook page organized around a Florida community and a local high school. It was a virtual reunion of the class of 1968 and they were all in touch with one another after many years of going their separate ways.

Sheryl, who was born at the tag end of the boomer years and looks more like a postgraduate student than one of the most powerful executives of the Internet era, laughed when she described an early meeting at Facebook. The executive team was discussing a new launch when one said, "Well, we have to take into account all user demographics," and then, waving at Sheryl, added, "including the middle-aged."

Sheryl at first didn't know who he was waving at, but she quickly made the story into a parable about Facebook as more than just a youthful fancy.

She said, "As you get older, the barriers of time and geography become more important and we have to break them down. Facebook does that with virtual reunions which, in turn, get more people to the real reunions."

When I asked if Facebook would replace the nursery song "Over the river and through the woods to grandmother's house we go," Sandberg responded quickly, "I don't think so, but Facebook makes it easier to share on a daily basis. We hear stories of people getting to watch their grandkids take their first step on video on Facebook."

There is another, unexpected, surge in social networking by baby boomers desperate to find answers to a challenge they had not anticipated: caring for their elderly parents, many of whom have lived into their late eighties or nineties. They may be afflicted with dementia or Alzheimer's disease, and their boomer children are lighting up the Internet, looking for help or sharing stories. It's the electronic equivalent of a support group without the need to leave your keyboard.

Not all senior citizens are enthusiastic about Facebook and other social networking sites. At a Stanford University symposium called Generation Ageless: Longevity and the Boomers, a roundtable about the challenges and opportunities for America's growing senior population, Sheryl Sandberg was on a panel that included former U.S. Supreme Court justice Sandra Day O'Connor.

When I asked O'Connor if she stayed in touch with her former law clerks, she said, "Not as much as I'd like; I'm not sure where many of them are now." Sandberg seized the moment, saying, "We can find them on Facebook."

Justice O'Connor quickly made it clear she wasn't interested. "I don't need any more publicity, even on Facebook, definitely no!" She did admit, however, she likes to communicate with her grandchildren on Skype, the video teleconference website and software.

The Internet, with or without Facebook, can be the best kind of common ground for generation-to-generation bonding. Our fourteen- and twelve-year-old granddaughters, Claire and Meredith, routinely share with us interesting or amusing sites on the Internet and we send them suggestions on what to look up. When Claire spent a school holiday in Nicaragua we exchanged impressions of the country via email.

Sometimes the Internet is an unexpected meeting place for our two widely separated generations. On the weekend of my birthday I took the girls to a rehearsal of **Saturday Night Live** at NBC when the teen heartthrob Ashton Kutcher was guest host.

When he appeared onstage to walk through a sketch Claire immediately whipped out her smartphone and began typing furiously. When I asked what she was up to, she said, impatiently, "Tom, I'm texting all my friends about this monumental moment." Later Kutcher kindly came over to say hello and asked what had brought us all together. When the girls said it was my seventieth birthday, he raised his eyebrows and said, "Seventy? I don't believe it." Although I am not a teenage girl I was ready to sign up for his fan club.

In the cab ride home, my phone buzzed and I learned from friends that Kutcher had tweeted the same message. "I just met Tom Brokaw. It's his 70th birthday. He doesn't look a day over 50!" Now my granddaughters were doubly impressed because Kutcher is the king of Twitter, with more followers than any other young star.

I thought back to my teenage years and how exciting it would have been to have tweeted my friends and parents from the loge in Ebbets Field when I fulfilled a lifelong dream of seeing my beloved Dodgers in their home park the summer they were decamped to the West Coast by the O'Malley family—or the Saturday night I saw **Rebel Without a Cause** and instinctively knew that all-American boys in crew cuts and letter jackets were about to become passé with teenage girls.

The Kutcher experience is repeated millions of times a day around the globe, one hopes on more meaningful terms. It will only become an even larger part of our human experience, and it will make our world a neighborhood of social connections. But the test will be the constructive payoff of those connections: Will they enhance world understanding, promote justice and human rights, or help to organize a global response to issues such as climate change or infectious diseases? I believe you can do all of that and still meet a mate online, tweet about a new video, or buy a used tractor.

THE PROMISE

These are all tools that require an active intelligence and a fired-up imagination. These new tools must be an extension of our hearts and minds as well as our thumbs and impulses. Thankfully, a number of cyber whiz kids are already doing that. Microsoft has an alumni association that every year recognizes the innovative work of Microsoft graduates in the social sector.

Asked to help judge the 2010 competition, I was hard-pressed to single out just one or two efforts. They were uniformly impressive and addressed issues that heretofore had received too little attention.

William Brindley and Frank Schott work together on NetHope, which can best be described as a central command center for disparate international humanitarian organizations. When a disaster occurs—for example, the Haiti earthquake—NetHope sends teams of technologists to help with communication.

They set up Wi-Fi hot spots, satellite dishes, and solar generators and arrange for Skype vouchers so the participating NGO relief teams have access to reliable information and a means of coordinating with one another on the greatest needs of the area.

Chris Hughes, a cofounder of Facebook, is investing his time and a piece of his considerable fortune in an online venture called Jumo that he established to connect individuals and corporations with charities.

Hughes took the basic model of Facebook and applied it to Jumo, so nonprofits could establish pages and reach constituencies that might otherwise not know about their work, whether that's building a school in Africa or providing tutors to the inner city.

When the Middle East exploded with populist rage in the first quarter of 2011 the rebels were able to mobilize millions of like-minded oppressed citizens on Twitter and Facebook. Autocrats everywhere took notice: They could no longer divide and conquer an aggrieved population that now had access to a common and swift form of communication.

These are just a few of the innovative uses of this wide-ranging technology for the greater good. All of the giants of Silicon Valley and beyond—Google, Apple, Facebook, Microsoft, Yahoo!—have programs and personnel dedicated to finding solutions to substandard education, medical problems, and social needs. As an entrepreneurial class, the men and women of cyberspace are fearless and confident they can do anything.

Look at what they've done so far. We should all be cheering them on for what they'll do next. The advantages of technology are all around us. A few notable examples:

Agriculture: The National Academy of Sciences calculated that at the beginning of the twentieth century 38 percent of the labor force was needed for farmwork. By the turn of the twenty-first century, that number had fallen to 3 percent. Moreover, farming is so much more efficient as a result of animal genetics, plant biology, soil conservation, and innovation in machinery that less land is required to grow food for many more people worldwide.

Energy conservation: In the 1990s manufacturing output in the United States expanded by 41 percent but industrial consumption of electricity grew by only 11 percent. In the past four decades the U.S. economy has expanded by more than 126 percent yet technology has made it possible to expand electrical use by only 30 percent.

Medicine: Google or Bing the subject "medical technology" and up come pages from the highly regarded **Scientific American** or Science Daily websites with articles on new drugs, the effects of radiation, global cancer rates, the latest in aging research, and trends in sports medicine, as well as more complex subjects such as positron emission tomography.

Within the health care system nationally and globally technology makes possible diagnostic, surgical, and medical treatment that was unimaginable twenty years ago. A patient in Mumbai may be examined by a specialist in Boston without either leaving her home city.

That's a microscopic snapshot of both the work that is being done as a result of technology in medicine and the ability of laypersons to become more informed.

In medicine, particularly, it can work both ways. The anxious patient may find ailments on the Internet to fit his or her imagination and the physician may spend many more office hours trying to sort through a do-it-yourself diagnosis on the part of the ailing Internet enthusiast.

As our doctor daughter says, "We need more of the old-fashioned, sensible, grandmotherly advice to go with the modern technology."

CHAPTER 13

Everyone's a Journalist

FACT: According to the Newspaper Association of America, daily newspapers penetrate more than 55 percent of the population fifty-five years of age and older, almost 53 percent of potential readers thirty-five and older, but less than 33 percent of the population eighteen to thirty-four years of age.

Newspapers have lost an estimated 25 percent of their circulation since the turn of the twenty-first century.

Network evening news broadcasts on NBC, CBS, and ABC still deliver a lot of tonnage in terms of viewers—almost twenty-five million combined on an average weeknight—but they're also losing viewers to the proliferation of cable news outlets and, especially, websites, either those produced independently or by traditional newspaper publishers.

QUESTION: Where do you get your news on a daily basis? If it is a website, do you know who is providing the content? Are you more or less inclined to believe what you read on the Internet than what you pick up from elsewhere?

Wherever I appear—before civic groups, at conferences on a variety of issues, or at corporate gatherings—I know one question will arise: "What's happened to American journalism? Why is it all shouting and confrontation? Why can't we return to the days of Walter Cronkite and **The Huntley-Brinkley Report**?" As soon as the question is asked, the audience either applauds in support of the premise or leans forward in anticipation of the answer.

I welcome the opportunity, because I am eager to engage any audience in a wider discussion about the role of readers and viewers—citizens, if you will—on the health and form of the means by which they get the information on which they'll make decisions about their everyday lives and the future of their country.

We live in an information-rich environment. Never have there been so many choices available to news consumers. When the economics of the daily newspaper business first began to change and only deep-pockets enterprises remained, there was widespread consternation about the power of the sole surviving papers.

THE PAST

The New York Times, The Washington Post, and **The Wall Street Journal** were America's most powerful newspapers in the post–World War II era. They represented the crown jewels of daily American journalism, and it seemed it would be that way forever.

The **Los Angeles Times** in the sixties, seventies, and early eighties was the King Kong of Southern California journalism. Minneapolis was dominated by the **Star Tribune,** a morphing of two separate papers, one morning and one evening, owned by the same company.

Residents of San Francisco, a sophisticated city with bawdy newspapers, had two choices—the **Chronicle** and the **Examiner**—but the **Chronicle** prevailed when the **Examiner** was sold to an entrepreneur who turned it into a small broadsheet tabloid.

Then the world of print came under assault from all sides on the new fields of instantly accessible information. Highly profitable enterprises, including the venerated **New York Times** and **Washington Post,** were hit hard and scrambled to find a way to fit into the new realities.

Gannett, the national chain of small-market papers, moved into medium-sized cities and consolidated their properties. As the economic squeeze of the Great Recession began to choke off ad revenue, Gannett forced employees to take furloughs and instructed local papers to reprint the front page of the chain's flagship, **USA Today.**

Newspapers first came under assault from all-news cable television channels: MSNBC, CNBC, Fox News, Bloomberg, and the expanded spectrum of ESPN attaching themselves to the established worldwide orbit of CNN.

The Internet came right behind, with an explosive impact. At first dismissed as a solely academic tool by the likes of Bill Gates and other forefathers of the personal computer age, the Net quickly created a vast new universe of news and information.

The pressure on the traditional economic models of newspapers, especially big-city papers, was suffocating. One statistic sums up the economic crisis in traditional print journalism: At the beginning of the twenty-first century, print ad revenue brought in almost $49 billion to newspapers. By 2010, that number had fallen to almost $23 billion, a drop of 53 percent.

The **Seattle Post-Intelligencer** gave up print editions in favor of an online-only outlet. **The Boston Globe** went on life support. The Minneapolis **Star Tribune** filed for bankruptcy. The **Chi-**

cago **Tribune** and the **Los Angeles Times** wound up in the hands of a real estate developer who railed against traditional journalistic practices and promised big changes, but instead lost big money. **The New York Times,** after an uncertain start, revamped its electronic editions and charged subscribers for access. The Good Gray Lady was suddenly ablaze with blogs and snazzy graphics, gossipy items and more commentary. The **Times** also became a wine and archival photograph vendor.

THE PRESENT

The Second Big Bang is not yet complete, and may never be finished, given the pace of information evolution. However, some patterns are beginning to emerge. Traditional print and electronic journalism is finding new life on the digital spectrum. Newspaper, magazine, and television news enterprises are constantly refining their content-delivery systems so that print, over-the-air, and cable news can all move seamlessly to the websites in an appealing fashion, easily accessible on cellphones or other personal digital appliances such as the iPad.

Old-line print reporters and editors looked at the road ahead and saw a cliff, so a number of them jumped to the Internet with a new form of journalism.

When Rupert Murdoch's News Corporation took over **The Wall Street Journal,** the paper's managing editor, Paul Steiger, left for online journalism. Steiger put together a nonprofit online investigative journalism site called ProPublica in 2008, and within three years it had won two Pulitzer Prizes. Not a bad start for a newsroom with only thirty-four reporters.

Gawker, an aggressive, take-no-prisoners website run by Nick Denton, who relishes his bad-boy reputation, is the antithesis of what once passed for high-church journalism. Denton believes in giving readers what they want, and he goes to almost any length to get the inside scoop on juicy scandals or simply outrageous behavior. Denton told James Fallows in an **Atlantic** magazine profile that he's most annoyed by what he described as "the pompous liberals . . . with their endless handwringing" in the American media.

The Huffington Post, managed by the enterprising Arianna Huffington, was an early high-profile success. It was established as an antidote to the conservative and lively Drudge Report. When AOL bought the HuffPost, as it's known, Huffington pocketed a cool $100 million and kept control of the content.

When the always inventive Steve Jobs gave the world the iPad, the electronic tablet, the always opportunistic Rupert Murdoch quickly came up with a newspaper, The Daily, to be sold and downloaded to iPad users. Two years earlier, at a Seattle conference, I had watched Murdoch swarm all over Jeff Bezos, the founder of Amazon, inquiring about the possibility of using the Kindle, Amazon's e-book reader, as an outlet for a new form of journalism. At the time I thought, This could be the accomodation my generation has been looking for: a larger print and page format and yet still portable.

Washington quickly took to another electronic enterprise. Politico, a site devoted to all things political, was instantly a popular aggregator of political gossip, hard news, commentary, and video, all assembled in the early morning by the indefatigable Mike "Mikey" Allen, a former print reporter who gained sudden fame and a lengthy profile in **The New York Times Magazine**. His work is an electronic version of the three-dot journalism perfected by the legendary newspaper columnists Walter Winchell, Irv Kupcinet in Chicago, and the peerless Herb Caen in San Francisco.

When Ronald Reagan was first running for governor of California and still primarily thought of as an actor, Caen wrote in one of his columns, "I had a dream it was election night and the television cameras cut to a stage with a heavy velvet curtain in Southern California as an offscreen voice said, 'Now accepting for Ronald Reagan in Los Angeles, here's Greer Garson.' " Dot. Dot. Dot.

It was a funny line and perfect for Herb's liberal San Francisco readership at the time, but as he always seemed to, the Gipper got the last laugh. In 2011, the nation celebrated what would have been Reagan's one hundredth birthday with a series of galas and symposia in which he was widely hailed as a great and transformative president.

Online news portals, whether it is Cleveland .com—dedicated to covering local news in Cleveland—Slate, or Salon, all seem to have the same DNA. They're breezy with colorful graphics and a kind of pinball machine energy. They promote reader polls on popular topics.

Lindsay Lohan, jail or no jail?

Would you buy a ticket to a Mel Gibson movie?

Should smoking be banned in the United States? Vote yes or no and check the results.

These are not scientific polls, but they have a certain allure for readers who want some indication their voice is being heard.

Local online newspapers drop the drawbridge across the moat and invite everyone in. Be a reporter, urges Cleveland.com. Send us your video—a standard practice for nearly all the online enterprises.

A site called WikiLeaks became a nuclear reactor of online journalism in the late autumn of 2010 when it released thousands of pages of secret government documents to **The New York Times,** the Manchester **Guardian,** and a few other select publications. WikiLeaks in turn had gotten the documents electronically from a private first class who plainly had more unmonitored access to sensitive material than might be expected for someone so young and so low in rank.

Suddenly, newspapers, broadcast and cable outlets, bloggers, and electronic and print magazines had the journalistic equivalent of an oil gusher: a vast pool of U.S. government cables and memos describing everything from the prospects of an Iranian nuclear weapon to the sexual appetites of Moammar Gadhafi.

Public editors and radio talk show hosts praised, damned, and analyzed the leaks as government officials expressed public outrage but privately sighed in relief that the leaks weren't more embarrassing.

Bottom line: The news consumer can no longer be a couch potato, content to pick the morning paper off the front porch, check drive-time radio for weather and traffic, dip into the first hour of the **Today** show or any of the other network breakfast offerings, keep an eye on CNN or MSNBC or CNBC or FOX during the day, and try to catch the **NBC Nightly News** or ABC or CBS in the early evening.

That does not even include the popular Internet sites and cable networks of foreign news outlets, ranging from Al Jazeera in English to the BBC World Service to Xinhuanet, a news site produced by Xinhua, the official press agency of China, out of offices in Times Square in New York. The fastest-growing part of the American ethnic strata is Latino or Hispanic, the preferred nomenclature changing from region to region. Whatever the shorthand, Spanish-language cable outlets and radio stations are now a fixed and important part of the spectrum, serving an audience estimated to be nearing fifty million in the United States in the next decade.

THE PROMISE

Information is moving too swiftly and emanating from too many directions and sources for a citizen to be well informed as just a casual observer. Moreover, there are cleverly designed sites and commentaries that give the impression of journalism when in fact they're little more than propaganda forums or commercial product forums.

However, with a little enterprise, the average citizen in the most remote part of the country is capable of being as well informed as the most sophisticated and educated urban dweller, if he or she is adventurous and vigilant. The adventure comes with the realization that the Internet and cable networks can now take you inside a vast vault of cultural, political, economic, and historic information with a keystroke or channel flip; the vigilance grows out of the same skepticism that compels us to research options before purchasing a new flat-screen television or automobile or insurance policy. In the modern age of news dissemination, more than ever before, it is "consumer beware." Cleverness or bells-and-whistle packaging alone doesn't equal reliability or integrity.

Some outlets will pander to your fears or offer commentary designed to reaffirm your anxieties. They provide false comfort, and they represent the full arc of the political spectrum. They're designed to constantly divide and conquer rather than attempt to find common ground on which to move forward.

They have a place in a free society, but as Bill Clinton, the first president subjected to the full force of the electronic news feeding frenzy, put it, "There's no sort of home base for what's accurate or not. I worry about the atomizing of our society and creating an almost attention deficit disorder. We want to know everything right now. We want everything done right now. We want to make an opinion right now. And then we want to act on it, right now."

The numbers underscore his concerns. In 1990, total circulation of newspapers was 62.3 million; by 2010, it had fallen to 43.4 million. In 2000, 46 percent of the adult population used the Internet; by 2010, it was 79 percent. Furthermore, in 2010, 41 percent of Americans said they got their news from an Internet source, and 42 percent said they got their news from two to six platforms a day. Already many of those electronic platforms have proven their reliability for accuracy and integrity, but the opportunity for mischief, malicious and otherwise, is almost unlimited.

News consumers can no longer be couch potatoes. We all have to work much harder at determining the source, motivation, and long-term credibility of our news sources.

Clinton, who has been called the baby boomer in chief by columnist David Brooks, had another concern: "One excess that the baby boomers had on both sides of the Vietnam and cultural divide was a tendency to sanctimony. If you get too sanctimonious it makes you really dumb, because you can't hear anything anymore. Maybe one of the things we can do is give the American people the space to listen to each other across these divides again."

Journalism is not a craft I am personally willing to surrender to the dividers.

As long as readers and viewers will give me the benefit of their attention, I will continue the work that has been so gratifying to me in all the forms now available. The selfish reasons are self-evident: Journalism is just so interesting and constantly changing, from the small-town police beat to the highest councils of government and inner sanctums of distant cultures. It is a license to turn over rocks, look around corners, engage anyone with something important or merely entertaining to say, to give voice to the voiceless and to correct wrongs.

One of the most damaging consequences of the decline in economics for newspapers is the diminishing place of investigative journalism. It's estimated that in the past ten years, newspapers—and that means the largest and most influential—have cut back their investigative staffs by at least 30 percent.

Allow me to remind us all of one essential truth: The forms of journalism may be changing and the clatter and clutter may be more cacophonous, but the importance of journalism—the light it shines and the oxygen it provides—is indispensible. Without journalism, what would we know of the people's revolt in Egypt, or, long before that, of Watergate? My Lai? The Silent Spring? AIDS? Iran-Contra? Tiananmen Square? War, Islamic rage, nuclear proliferation, peace, calamity, and heroism?

The place of journalism practiced rigorously and ethically has always transcended the noisy presence of false prophets and exploiters, and I would like to continue to play a role in preserving that legacy for as long as I am vertical. I have adopted the terse response of my friend Andy Rooney, who, when asked when he would retire, responded in that endearingly gruff fashion he's made so famous, "Retire from **what**? **Life**?"

CHAPTER 14

Partners

FACT: One of the indelible and patently fallacious American myths is that of the heroic lone gunman riding into town to save the local law-abiding citizens from the evils of a villain with a black heart and a hat to match. Matt Dillon had Chester. The Lone Ranger always had Tonto. Wyatt Earp didn't go to the O.K. Corral on his own; he had the help of his brothers and Doc Holliday.

QUESTION: Is life more complicated now? From time to time, one of the Internet sites will pose that question and get a wide range of answers, from "Yes! And I'm going back to 1957" to "Are you kidding? Think of how much easier it is to find something on the Internet instead of going to the library, or to take your favorite music with you everywhere on a small device." It really does come down to different strokes for different folks, but the big choices in life seem to be more complicated. There was a time when you could take a job with a big company and if you did reasonably well you'd become a lifer, working at the same place until retirement.

You had a company pension or retirement program with health benefits. You were able to pay off a mortgage. You could have a small business on Main Street and support your family because you didn't have to worry about Walmart setting up a superstore on the edge of town. You could see your friendly physician and he (for it was almost always a man) would have time to discuss your case personally, and maybe refer you to a friend who was a specialist, and your insurance covered it all, no questions asked. You get the picture.

Now, all day long, choices, choices, choices, and how to decide which count and which don't?

THE PRESENT

The rapid rise of social networking on computers and smartphones is another sign of how swiftly our world is changing. At first I dismissed it as an electronic form of junior high note passing and wondered why I had to have new "friends" letting me know their latest thoughts. After all, I have trouble enough keeping up with the long roll call of email that demands my attention every waking hour, wherever I am in the world.

The popularity of social networking should not be a surprise in a culture where everyone seems to be surgically attached to some kind of cellphone all day and into the night. One study determined that 90 percent of Americans with cellphones were constantly within three feet of them. A Stanford law student stopped me as I was walking across that campus and said, "Mr. Brokaw, you've written about other generations. What about our generation? We seem to be redefining the meaning of 'friend' without understanding what real friendship means."

In a play on Descartes's timeless observation "I think, therefore I am," we now are a society that proclaims "I'm online, therefore I am."

No one understood that better than Barack Obama, who became the first truly online all-star presidential candidate. He had profiles on fifteen different social networks, including not just Facebook but also networks tying together Asian, Hispanic, African, and other ethnic groups.

At its peak the My.BarackObama.com website had eight and a half million monthly visitors—that is, prospective voters who went to the trouble of finding his website and exploring it.

Just as the television ad once changed the presidential campaign, the digital age with all of its current and future variations means that no prospective voter can escape detection. Beyond politics and commerce, it's difficult to quantify just how much of the messaging is at best vapid. Twitter accounts don't come with a twaddle alert.

But I have become persuaded that social networking represents something deeper than just staying in touch. Consciously and unconsciously it is an acknowledgment that the world is a more complicated place and it is better to have several minds working on a problem than one. Pick any area of everyday life and compare it to the routines of, say, thirty years ago.

Grocery shopping is now an exercise in reading the fine print on the content label: Can it really have that much sodium? Is this bottle made from recycled material and can it be redeemed? Gone are the days when you went to the family physician and did whatever he said. Should I buy the hybrid car or wait for the electric plug-in? Why can't I get into this public school? I live here!

Now, go to the next level of decision making. Do

I wait until I am forty to have a baby? Will I ever be able to pay off this second mortgage or student debt or pay for my mother who needs live-in care at age ninety-one and whose doctor says she'll probably live to be one hundred? What's the family plan if there's another terrorist attack?

THE PAST

I often think back to my days as a waterfront instructor at a Boy Scout summer camp.

When it was time for a group swim, the buddy system went into effect. You swam with a buddy and watched each other. When I blew the whistle, every pair of swimmers had to raise joined hands so I could see that no one was missing. I didn't realize it at the time, but life is richer and problems are easier if you have a buddy.

There are manifold examples, large and small, through history, none more telling than Winston Churchill and Franklin Roosevelt leading the Western alliance to victory in World War II, two men from aristocratic families with a common capacity to mobilize their spoken language as a fighting force. They also shared a ravenous appetite for the challenges of public service when the stakes for their countries could not have been higher.

President Roosevelt is said to have commented to Churchill at the beginning of their joint effort to defeat Germany and Japan, "I love sharing this decade with you."

In turn, they were married to strong, smart women who knew when to nudge their spouses back from their excesses, not always successfully but often just enough to keep their reputations intact and their policies on track.

In my lifetime there have been so many examples of partners not just complementing each other but creating a whole greater than their two parts. What would Hewlett have been without Packard, Huntley without Brinkley, McCartney without Lennon, Woodward without Bernstein? Butch without Sundance, Redford without Newman?

And vice versa for all.

Partners range from the laboratories to the playing fields.

Francis Crick and James Watson worked together to crack the DNA code, one of the most important scientific achievements, ever. Larry Page and Sergey Brin met as students at Stanford and teamed up to create Google. Joe Montana was my idea of the best all-time National Football League quarterback, but without Jerry Rice, who knows?

Fred Astaire was a portrait of grace on his own but with Ginger Rogers in his arms he soared beyond whatever the choreographer had in mind. As my former NBC colleague Linda Ellerbee so pointedly put it, "Ginger Rogers did everything Fred Astaire did and she did it in high heels while dancing backward." (The late Texas governor Ann Richards used the quote so often she got credit for originating it, but it was Linda's first.)

This lesson in the importance of productive partnerships and the often dissonant qualities that produce them came into personal focus for me during one of the most difficult assignments of my reporting career: Watergate.

I was the White House correspondent for NBC News, all but surgically attached to the White House press room from the summer of 1973 to August 1974, when Richard Nixon became the first American president forced to resign the office.

It was a tense and demanding assignment for a journalist and nothing short of a constitutional crisis for the country. America was transformed into a vast courtroom filled with citizens suddenly confronted with the possibility their president was a crook, despite his emphatic denials. The legal arguments were often complex and the political battles were nothing short of hand-to-hand combat for the most powerful piece of real estate in the world, the Oval Office.

I'd arrive at the press room early and leave late every day that we weren't traveling to Russia, Paris,

Florida for the weekend, or Nixon rallies in Arizona and at Walt Disney World. To many in those audiences, still faithful to the president, the White House press corps, not Richard Nixon, was the enemy. Others wanted us to simply proclaim him guilty and throw him out.

Sometime in the fall of 1973 I struck up a friendship with a fellow Midwesterner, Fred Zimmerman of **The Wall Street Journal** by way of Kansas City. We were an unlikely pair. He was a chess whiz and a laconic newspaperman. I was a gregarious television journalist without the patience for the intricacies of chess. We shared a passion for cool jazz and the American literature of our generation. We sat side by side on long trips and ended long days with Scotch on the rocks.

The friendship evolved. We compared notes daily and shared information and impressions. On rare lunch outings we'd order hamburgers and chew over the latest White House machinations. Often I'd say, "Fred, what they did today just doesn't make sense." Fred would look up from his burger, arch an eyebrow, and say, "Until you remember he's guilty."

Oh, yeah, that. But we never allowed each other to go into print or on the air with that proclamation. We knew not just the presidency was at stake but also the reputation of American journalism. Fred had my back and I had his.

Fred's reputation as a meticulous reporter helped

get him through an ordeal that was at once hilari-
ous and bizarre. Shortly after President Nixon told
a Walt Disney World audience in the fall of 1973,
"I'm not a crook," he went outside to work the rope
line of lined-up spectators who were hoping to
shake his hand.

One was a burly Air Force sergeant there with his
daughter. In a completely Nixonian moment, the
president leaned over, greeted the little girl, and
then looked up into the lights at the sergeant and
said, "Are you the girl's mother?" The startled Air
Force veteran said, "No, I'm her father!"

Nixon, now realizing his mistake, said, "Of
course you are," and reached up to pat the man's
face, but in his typical physical clumsiness, the pat
became a slap. The sergeant was dumbfounded and
Nixon moved on.

Fred was the pool reporter, representing the rest
of the White House press, and he dutifully and in
a straightforward way reported the incident to the
rest of us. The White House press office went bal-
listic, denying it had happened. Because it was
Fred, the rest of us believed it, and later the sergeant confirmed Fred's account.

You see? Watergate wasn't all constitutional arguments.

Fred and I have stayed in touch. He's long been
retired from **The Wall Street Journal** and is now a

scholar of classic Greek history and language at the University of North Carolina, one more example of our different interests. However, when we occasionally get together we quickly rediscover the rhythms of our relationship and fall into spirited discussions about what is going on in the world.

From those White House days forward I have examined successful enterprises through a different prism. More often than not, there is a thriving partnership at work even if one of the partners is much less visible than the other.

Ronald Reagan was one of the most successful American politicians of the twentieth century and yet for all of his obvious personal skills he was helped immeasurably by two strong partners. One was his wife, Nancy, who was tenacious and insightful in protecting and promoting her husband's career and public image. The other was his first chief of staff, James Baker, scion of a Houston banking and law firm family. Baker had worked for his friend George H. W. Bush in his 1980 primary campaign against Reagan. It was Nancy's idea to bring Baker over to their side when Reagan won the election. It was a brilliant choice, with Baker keeping a low profile as he fine-tuned the daily and long-term White House operations so Reagan could be Reagan, the masterful player on the big stage.

Martin Luther King, Jr., is a towering figure in

American history, with a legacy that can be summed up in one sweeping sentence: He liberated America, white as well as black, from the shameful shackles of segregation. The power of his oratory, his commitment to a philosophy of nonviolence, and his faith in the rule of law were three pillars of his enduring achievement. Dr. King also depended on the legal skills of Thurgood Marshall, later the first African American to become a justice of the U.S. Supreme Court. Within the civil rights movement, the quiet managerial efficiencies of Andrew Young, the boyish son of a New Orleans dentist, kept the focus on the larger goal.

THE PROMISE

Anne Mulcahy and Ursula Burns are the first chairwoman and the first female CEO of a Fortune 500 company, and their unique standing atop Xerox is a tribute to their individual skills but also to their shared views and experiences as women, mothers, and wives in a space heretofore reserved mostly for men. As they rose through the ranks of Xerox, they didn't spend Monday morning comparing Saturday's golf scores but instead talked about how to fit day care and matrimonial priorities into their already crowded schedules.

I have spent more than forty-five years in a col-
legial profession, journalism. While I've been in
front of the camera, the audiences couldn't see the
producers, cameramen and women, film and video
editors, researchers, and technicians who always
knew something I didn't: how the picture got from
where I worked to where you saw it. To me it was
magic, and I left it at that.

Broadcast journalism is an intensely personal
business, in that we bump up against one another
all day long, all over the world, in war zones and
garden spots alike. We work through the night in
distant time zones and watch each other's backs in
hostile neighborhoods. I could not have had even a
small measure of whatever success I've achieved
without these brothers and sisters doing the heavy
lifting behind the scenes wherever the news took
us, but there was another partner as well on what
came to be called Team Brokaw: Meredith, my
partner of almost a half century.

She's modest, controlled, understated, and gifted
in the precision arts such as bridge, knitting, cooking, and horseback riding. She's been a successful
retailer and author. Meredith is also musical and
has a keen eye for the strengths and weaknesses of
novels.

She's married to a man who has spent their married life in one corner of the vanity business, not

immune to the trappings of celebrity. His one brief pass at bridge was described by an instructor as "cowboy," and his musical tone deafness is legendary within the family.

Apart from her willingness to still laugh at my jokes, her greatest strength has been as a female role model for our three daughters and as a woman not at all dependent on her husband's lowercase celebrity. I am not kidding when people ask how my wife deals with my public role and I respond, "When I get home at night it's a relief when Meredith remembers what I do for a living."

We've been fortunate through our long marriage to almost always be in the right place at the right time—a serendipitous fate—but we've also managed to be more than the sum of our parts, an unexpected dividend we could not have imagined when we fell in love almost a half century ago. We're not so **dependent** on each other as we are **complementary** in our relationship, a critical difference.

PART FOUR

What Now, Grandma and Grandpa?

CHAPTER 15

Balancing the Book of Life

FACT: When Richard Nixon opened the door to China in 1972, the Chinese were living a nineteenth-century way of life and were in the midst of a cruel so-called Cultural Revolution, Mao Zedong's attempt to reignite the fires of Communist passion. Less than half a century later, China has become the second-largest economy in the world, pressing for number one, and scholars are projecting that the twenty-first century will be for China what the twentieth was for the United States.

QUESTION: Are you ready to concede the title?

THE PAST

After almost a half century as a journalist I have an abiding faith in the wisdom of the American people to get it right for the long haul. I've been on the streets of urban and rural America when I thought violent racism and rage against a distant war might so shatter us that we would not be healed for generations to come. I had a close-up view of a felonious president taking the republic to the edge of a constitutional crisis before he was forced to resign. Other presidents tested the limits of their power and the patience of the voters with their personal failings or political hubris, inadequacies, and grave misjudgments.

In what may have been the most consequential confrontation in history, we won the Cold War and helped manage the largely peaceful breakup of the Soviet Union, a monumental achievement. Conversely, we were completely unprepared for the deadly realities of Islamic rage, and for more than a decade we've been struggling to find an effective response.

We have a challenge of a similar if not greater magnitude in filling the sinkhole that opened suddenly and swallowed whole sectors of the economy, exposing the fatal frailties of venerated financial institutions, ripping away the foundation of the American Dream—home ownership— and exposing the folly that the boom would go on forever.

We've recovered from every one of the earlier

assaults on what our forefathers called "the general welfare of the people" because of the resilience of the citizens of this immigrant nation. Even in the darkest moments, wisdom and resolve crossed class lines, from blue-collar communities to the paneled halls of our most elite institutions.

There are new realities now for America that cannot be vanquished solely with the comforting thought "We're still the greatest country in the world. We'll get out of this somehow." In fact, it will require more than national pride.

When we emerged from other recessions in the 1980s and '90s, we did not have China and India coming up fast on the inside track. The historic advances of China can be summed up in one startling statistic: In 2005, China's economy was half the size of Japan's, which at the time was the second largest in the world. By 2010, just five years later, China had passed Japan and had its sights fixed clearly on the United States as the number one global economy.

Moreover, in the earlier recoveries at the end of the twentieth century the baby boomers were at the peak of their spending power. Now they are entering the age of **taking** instead of spending, receiving Medicare and Social Security. As life spans are extended, who will take care of the parents and grandparents and at what cost?

THE PRESENT

Many voices are warning of the coming collision between expectations and costs in fulfilling the commitments of the so-called entitlement programs. Niall Ferguson, a Scottish-born Harvard professor of financial and economic history, is an outrider on this subject, shouting out to the aging herd of boomers, "What now?"

He puts their dilemma in stark terms. "There's been a very substantial number of people, coming up to retirement, who've had absolutely no income growth over the last ten or twenty years—white-collar and blue-collar alike."

Ferguson's speech cadence goes up a notch when he says, "Americans talk sometimes as if they don't have a welfare state. I find that bizarre! You have a huge welfare state in the form of Medicare and Social Security. The costs of these systems are completely out of control. While the prices of most things have come down in terms of inflation, the cost of health care for the elderly has been explosive."

Here are some numbers to keep in mind. Almost one-third of **all** Medicare expenditures every year go to the 5 percent of the beneficiaries who are afflicted with terminal illnesses or are dying of old age. So when health care costs are debated it is a cheap shot to attack necessary end-of-life discussions as "death panels for Grandma."

In Oregon, a state with a program for physician-assisted dying, a study found that patients who requested the advice of doctors were primarily interested in dying at home and being in control of their circumstances. Other studies have shown that dying patients who discuss their options openly with a physician account for about 60 percent less in costs in their final week of life, to say nothing of the emotional costs that are saved when the family is on board with the plan.

Apart from the end-of-life decisions, Ferguson likes to remind his students and others, "We have institutions set up for life expectancy closer to seventy than the mideighties and still we're organized to have people stop work in their early to midsixties."

If the arithmetic isn't changed, Ferguson warns, the United States will end up like a Latin American economy because our finances are permanently off-kilter. He reckons if nothing is done, the unfunded liabilities for Social Security and Medicare will reach $100 trillion by 2050.

Ferguson is part of a large chorus of people warning of the destructive effect of an aging population and an unreformed entitlements program. It's been the stuff of think tanks and academic abstracts for years. Former U.S. Commerce secretary Peter Peterson has been a nag on the subject for as long as his friends can remember. When he finally cashed out on Wall Street, he set aside a considerable chunk of his fortune to make the public more aware of the long-term consequences of delaying resolution until an uncertain date in the future.

It's a subject that appears regularly on the Sunday talk shows and in opinion columns. Major health care delivery systems, such as the Mayo Clinic and the Cleveland Clinic, warn they won't be able to remain economically healthy if Medicare isn't reformed for the long haul. Nonetheless, the subject has been politically radioactive because older generations of recipients are militant defenders of the status quo.

It wasn't until the spring of 2011 that the debate took a new turn when Republican congressman Paul Ryan of Wisconsin, a politician with the face of a choirboy and the resolve of a Marine drill sergeant, proposed a radical new plan and forced a vote in the House of Representatives.

Ryan's proposal touched off an immediate backlash from Medicare recipients and leading Republicans quietly took a step back, but it was the prelude to an even larger, more divisive battle to come over how to reduce the national debt.

By July 2011, President Obama and congressional Republicans and Democrats were in an ugly, drawn-out fight over a plan on how to cut federal spending. The contentious feud moved from the White House to the Capitol, from the cable networks to the editorial pages, back and forth for most of the month with the exchanges becoming more acrimonious with every passing day.

They were trying to formulate a plan of some kind before August 2, when the United States had to temporarily raise its debt limit so it could pay due bills. But the far larger influence was the Tea Party Republicans in the House and Senate who would not be moved on the issue of raising additional revenue in any form to help with the balance sheet.

Tea Party members and their sympathizers did not represent a numerical majority in the Congress but through their determination and discipline they defined the debate and dictated the outcome.

The stumble-to-the-finish-line compromise was so patched together and the process was so maddening that America's creditworthiness was downgraded by S&P for the first time in U.S. history. That in turn set off wild gyrations in the markets.

Tea Party members put all the blame on the administration, further infuriating their critics. The larger political lesson, I think, is that the Tea Party demonstrated the power of discipline. As I said on **Meet the Press,** they played by the rules. They got angry, they got organized, and "they got here"—Washington, where they did exactly as promised. What that means for the long-term interests of the country and the political system will be a front-and-center issue in the 2012 presidential campaign.

A significant part of that debate will be the role of entitlement programs in our national future, rightly so.

The summer Meredith and I were married, 1962, her father's physician partners gave us a series of dinners and the discussion was often about the early stages of the Medicare debate in Congress. To a man, they were adamantly opposed. They reflected the view of the American Medical Association that it was an attempt by the government to take over medicine.

At the time, my beloved grandmother Ethel was beginning to have health problems that would eventually lead to long-term care. Neither she nor my parents had the financial resources to make that kind of a commitment, so I became the lone voice at the table advocating Medicare.

There I was, a brash twenty-two-year-old, not yet with a job, arguing with my future father-in-law and other pillars of the community that the least we can do as a society is take care of the elderly indigent when they become ill. Occasionally the discussions became pretty heated, so my mother took me aside and said, "If you don't shut up, Dr. Auld will call off this wedding."

Thankfully, he did not, and three years later Medicare passed, the backbone of what President Lyndon Johnson called his Great Society program. By modern standards, it was limited in scope. It did not cover doctor's visits or prescription drugs, long-term catastrophic care, or the many expensive procedures that became routine with the rapid advances in medical technology.

Still, it was a bonanza for the medical community. Physicians were guaranteed payment for treating a class of patients that had heretofore been a financially risky proposition: the elderly poor. In the early stages of the program doctors formed partnerships and opened X-ray and other testing centers to which they would refer their Medicare patients, a practice that gave them a double dip out of the payment system.

On the patient side, it was not just the elderly poor who benefitted. Wealthy Medicare recipients took full advantage of the program. A friend, one of the country's leading hand surgeons and a man interested in health care reform, was exasperated when he told me, "Some of my patients are among the richest people in the country and it's not unusual for them to say, 'I just want you to do what Medicare covers.'"

Personally I have long believed we have to apply greater means testing to Medicare, and based on informal surveys of well-to-do recipients the time to do it is now, given the stark financial consequences of not taking bold action soon.

We're rapidly approaching the time when hand-wringing, debate, and anxiety give way to paying the balance due for the crush of elderly boomers coming into the system.

Without reform, the American middle class, which represents the heart and arteries of the American economy and political culture, will be in a constant state of financial stress and anxiety. Elizabeth Warren, a Harvard law professor and architect of President Obama's Consumer Financial Protection Bureau, has another set of concerns about the continuing pressures on the middle class. Warren was chief adviser to the National Bankruptcy Review Commission and is the author of eight books on credit and economic stress.

Warren was a sharp critic of the original Troubled Asset Relief Program (TARP) initiated by

Treasury Secretary Henry Paulson and approved by a bipartisan vote of Congress in the closing frantic days of the Bush administration, when it seemed the world financial systems were about to collapse. To be fair, Paulson was operating without a net in emergency circumstances as he tried to keep some of the world's largest banks afloat with infusions of cash to be paid back once the crisis passed. The specter of a worldwide depression was not an exaggeration.

Paulson, the former CEO of Goldman Sachs, received high praise from most of the leading corporate and financial experts, who credited him with keeping the recession from tipping into a worldwide depression. Warren saw the bailout as one more example of rewarding the top while ignoring the middle, especially in the banking industry where most of the failures were small- and middle-sized banks.

Large financial institutions, such as Citibank, she argued, were not forced to go through bankruptcy or fire the people who made the mistakes in the first place, while taxpayers, who had their own economic stress, were made to bail out the big boys.

It is that kind of uneven treatment that arouses the ire of Warren, a native of Oklahoma who watched her middle-class father go broke because of predatory lending practices. It is not surprising that many powerful members of the financial services executive ranks are not fans of Warren, who constantly asks, "Why should the middle class, traditionally the heart of American society, undergo such strain?"

She's extensively studied two-income middle-class families and concluded that they have been trapped, first by the inflation that robbed the primary wage earner of any real gain, and then when the other parent or partner went to work they still couldn't keep up with the rising costs of housing, education, transportation, and big-ticket health care.

"When a middle-class family files for bankruptcy," she found, "it was often medical bills that forced the decision, not credit card debt."

Warren would like to see health care reform and more socially responsible banks and corporations on the U.S. landscape. So would one of the most powerful women in that rarefied world of paneled offices, chauffeured limousines, and private planes at the ready.

THE PROMISE

Indra Krishnamurthy Nooyi is a prominent member of the growing population of women breaking the old-boy culture in the executive offices of American corporations. Born and educated in India, she came to America to attend graduate school in business at Yale University. She worked first for business consulting firms before joining PepsiCo, where she ascended to the dual role of chairman and chief operating officer of the global soft drink and food powerhouse.

In that position she created a strategy called Performance with Purpose, a business plan for growth based on a healthier planet and healthier products.

Speaking to the Economic Club of Chicago, Nooyi got right to the crux of the problem that almost sank America during the Great Recession. "Capitalism," she said, "went right to the edge because of an excess of risk taking. Our capacity to understand the risks was outstripped by our ingenuity in devising new ones. Why were the risks taken? Because many were chasing short-term goals, short-term profitability, and short-term compensation. Many CEOs forgot they were trustees of an economic system."

That's a succinct summary of a disastrous course that almost ended with a calamitous crash.

Nooyi's solution?

"The first and most important thing we can do is to change our narrative about what companies are for and what they exist to do. As capitalists, we need to rediscover a higher calling."

She went on to explain how companies became

simply instruments to make money, lots of money, as swiftly as possible. "That's not a description of a company," she said, bluntly. "That's a caricature. A company is not an engine for the short term. It is a complex organism, and it does not float free of society, free of long-term obligations."

Turning to corporate leadership, Nooyi challenged corporate CEOs to "stress long-term gain even if it means short-term pain. We live in an age when trust has to be earned, not demanded. Institutions, public and private, now relate to individuals in a wholly new way."

Nooyi offered a new universe for the corporate world, which had become accustomed to being the sun god. "Today," she said, "the public are the golden globe at the center of the system. We, politicians and corporations, encircle them, trying to gain their attention and win their trust. We have to set out a clear path to a long-term future . . . to measure sustainable performance and capture the sense of a wider purpose."

Curiously, America's two largest soft drink companies—Coca-Cola and Pepsi—are run by foreign nationals. Muhtar Kent, the chairman and CEO of Coca-Cola, is a native of Turkey, a suave, international businessman who breathed new life into the many Coke enterprises after a succession of CEOs failed to maintain the success of the late

Roberto Goizueta, a Cuban-born entrepreneur who guided the soft drink behemoth for the final years of the twentieth century.

Kent stepped up Coke's recycling program and expanded its product line, significantly improving the profit margins. He also worked hard at good corporate citizenship. When Japan was devastated by the earthquake and tsunami, Kent immediately ordered thousands of cases of safe drinking water and other supplies shipped to the shattered areas, and he personally visited Japan to meet with Coca-Cola bottlers and other partners to see what they needed.

The most successful corporations of the twenty-first century will be those who recognize they're dealing with a global customer base that will measure the value of their products by more than the old standard of "Did I get a good deal on this?" A good deal will go well beyond price.

It will no longer be enough for a multinational corporation to put up a large, self-congratulatory billboard on the road between the airport and the city center of, say, Bangkok. Companies will have to be better citizens socially, environmentally, and culturally to go head-to-head with their competitors from around the globe.

I have no illusions that this is a "Kumbaya" moment for my generation and boomers. Despite the election and publicity victories of Tea Party activists, there will be no Reverend Moon–like ceremonies in basketball arenas and football stadia around the country with mass declarations to invoke Medicare more prudently and to delay activating Social Security payments until the age of seventy-five. The hotly engaged debate on government spending and taxes will not eradicate impulse shopping or spending beyond a family's means.

However, the Great Recession did force us to think anew about these issues, and for all the over-the-top rhetoric, the country came out of the painful downturn ready to put these questions on the table and act on them in a way that was not possible just a few years ago.

A place to begin: The more you have, the less you should get from the government in the way of entitlements. I have heard several well-off conservative friends say, "Look, I've worked hard and made enough money to take care of myself and my family. I don't think I should be running the bank on Medicare; I've made other arrangements for my health care." The time for an elevated means testing of Medicare, pegging benefits to income, is overdue.

Staggering retirement ages for Social Security

benefits is also an idea whose time has come. What grandparent of the future wants to explain to a granddaughter and a handful of her friends they have to work harder and contribute more so he can play golf every day at the age of sixty-two?

Furthermore, if this generation of grandparents wants to live up to its earlier promises and ideals it should also lead a new kind of wellness revolution. It would encompass not just a healthier lifestyle but also a more aggressive attitude toward the cost of health care.

I've taken to asking audiences and friends if they have any idea how much they spent last year on their personal health care. The reaction is almost always a sheepish, mumbling reply, "Er, uh, oh God, I have no idea." One prominent sports executive said to me, "I wouldn't even know where to ask." It is perpetually bewildering to me that in a society in which we haggle over automobile prices to the last decimal point, rush to catch the early bird special, show up only at happy hour, and tick off to friends and strangers alike how much we spent on a trip to New Orleans, for all of that, we have not a clue on how much we spent as a family out of pocket for health care.

Maybe every physician and clinic should have a sticker price in the window so we'd be forced to know.

As memories of the Great Depression died off with the generations that had lived through it, so did thrift as a badge of honor. "Spend today and who knows about tomorrow" became a national mantra. Magazines such as the **Robb Report** competed with one another in the celebration of personal wealth and the extravagant luxury it could buy. Bumper stickers popped up: "He who dies with the most toys wins."

That same attitude took hold in the public sector, from the highest levels of the federal government to the village green, fueled by boom times and careless stewardship. Republicans and Democrats alike treated public treasuries as bottomless ATMs, scattering cash across pet projects and buying off public employees unions and special interest groups with sweetheart deals, especially when it came to pensions. One of the many startling examples I came across in a casual survey of municipal retirement benefits involved the city of Los Angeles.

According to the **Los Angeles Times,** ten retired city water and power, fire and police employees will draw from $200,000 to $317,000 annually until they die. General David Petraeus, who commanded forces for a decade in Iraq and Afghanistan, will retire with a smaller pension than the bottom retiree on that **Los Angeles Times** list.

As a result of the public profligacy and the painful measures required to bring the budgets back into balance there is a rapidly expanding movement in the country with the shorthand PPP, which stands for public-private partnerships.

They take many forms, from private companies or nonprofit foundations helping individual schools or school systems by underwriting charter schools and community colleges to much larger projects such as funding transportation systems and roads.

Illinois and the neighboring state of Indiana are now connected by a privately run toll road. Two companies, one Australian and the other Spanish, teamed up to bid $1.8 billion to operate the Chicago Skyway toll road for ninety-nine years. They're responsible for operation and maintenance of the highway, which is a key link on the South Side of Chicago to expressways running east into Indiana.

For its part, Indiana sealed a deal with the same two companies for a 157-mile stretch of state highway running into the Chicago area. Indiana realized more than $3 billion in the deal, which has a seventy-five-year life span.

In both cases, the increases in tolls are limited to formulas governed by the consumer price index or the gross domestic product.

There are similar projects planned in Virginia, Colorado, and Texas and my guess is that more are coming, not just in transportation but also in water districts, public safety, technology, and economic development.

There are appropriate concerns that private companies managing or owning public sector enterprises will concentrate on the high end, leaving poor neighborhoods and their families to fend for themselves. Public labor union advocates raise questions about private labor practices in terms of wages and benefits. Thus far, most public-private partnerships seem to have addressed those issues in their contracts.

The savings and the efficiencies can be stupendous in some areas. Sioux City, Iowa, and neighboring communities—an area called Siouxland, in a corner of the country where Iowa, Nebraska, and South Dakota run together—had a common problem with wastewater from agriculture, food processing plants, and disconnected municipalities.

Enter Veolia Environmental Services, a nationally recognized water treatment company. Veolia has state-of-the-art systems and a profit incentive to stay atop the latest trends in technology and equipment. It entered into a compact with five communities representing a half million people in Siouxland to manage their wastewater discharges, and so far it has been a model of success.

The municipalities have saved almost $10 million since Veolia took over, and that doesn't count the additional revenue from the capture and reuse of methane gas from the discharges or the development of a local fertilizer industry from converted biosolids.

From wastewater to books, the trend is spreading. Dallas, Texas, approached the Kroger grocery store chain about a joint development in a library system in a Kroger-occupied shopping center. Kroger paid for the architectural design of the building and financed much of the construction.

It's paid off for the library system and for the grocery store chain. Library usage jumped almost 80 percent in the first two years of operation, and that increase in traffic was obviously a benefit at the Kroger checkout stands as well.

Southwest of Houston, in Fort Bend County, Texas, one of the fastest-growing areas in the country, the local economic development council has developed a keener understanding of what they have because of the Geographic Information System Technology, a system to map the area and provide instant access on a large touch-sensitive screen. Developers, companies, and government officials can stand together and get an immediate portrait of geography, demographics, tax structure, roads, utilities, and hazards in any given area.

As the Great Recession demonstrated, too often

painfully, there are many areas of the country that need to be reinvented—or at least renewed—and public-private partnerships on several levels and in a variety of forms will be a necessary and welcome part of positioning the country for the future.

CHAPTER 16

Failure Is an Option

FACT: In this age of "everyone knows everything about everyone," failures are hard to hide. Just ask former New York governor Eliot Spitzer, Nevada senator John Ensign, New York congressman Charles Rangel, former North Carolina senator and vice presidential candidate John Edwards, South Carolina governor Mark Sanford, evangelist Ted Haggard, actors Mel Gibson and Lindsay Lohan, or any number of other high-profile personalities who were outed for their indiscretions.

QUESTION: When was the last time you heard a prominent public or private leader who failed personally or professionally candidly acknowledge the mistakes and pledge to make the lessons learned a central part of the remainder of his or her life?

When the Great Recession hit and three of the most prestigious firms on Wall Street—Bear Stearns, Merrill Lynch, and Lehman Brothers—either disappeared or were rescued by other financial services companies, the men who ran them and got rich doing so became very defensive. They were seemingly incapable of saying, "Look, this happened on my watch. I screwed up and made some terrible decisions. I'm going to spend the rest of my days and a big chunk of my fortune helping those less fortunate than me. I've had the helicopters and country club memberships, the private plane awaiting me on the tarmac and the fifteen-hundred-dollar-a-night hotel suites. None of that gave me the judgment I should have had to head off these economic calamities."

THE PRESENT

Those executives and so many other politicians and celebrities caught in their own mistakes could use the lesson that played out across America in June 2010, from the playing field of the Detroit Tigers. Detroit pitcher Armando Galarraga was one out away from pitching a perfect game—no hits, no runs, no errors—one of baseball's most difficult feats.

A Cleveland Indians player hit a grounder to the Detroit first baseman, who made a quick throw to Galarraga, who rushed over to cover the bag. As he caught the ball, Galarraga broke into a big smile—a perfect game, a pitcher's dream!

But wait. Umpire Jim Joyce called the runner safe. Galarraga was stunned but walked back to the mound and retired the next batter as all the television replays showed that the batter on first had clearly been out.

After the game, umpire Joyce reviewed the video and knew that he made the wrong call. A veteran and highly respected ump, Joyce unconditionally acknowledged his error, saying, "I cost the kid a perfect game."

For the next twenty-four hours the blown call was replayed on all the cable channels and network news programs, rewatched on the Internet, and discussed on talk radio with a lot of intemperate comments about what should happen to umpire Joyce.

The following night at Tiger Stadium, Detroit manager Jim Leyland made a great call of his own. He asked Galarraga to present the night's lineup card to Joyce at the beginning of the game. Galarraga put his arm around Joyce and smiled as he handed over the card. Joyce teared up and the Detroit fans gave both men a standing ovation.

Detroit Tigers pitcher Armando Galarraga
and umpire Jim Joyce, the night after Joyce blew
a call and cost Galarraga a perfect game;
their emotional reunion was a lesson
that went well beyond a baseball game.

Once again our national pastime gave us a moment to remember and a simple but profound lesson in the virtues of acknowledging a mistake, forgiveness, and redemption.

It is not easy. We've all made large and small mistakes. None of us is perfect but again and again we fail to embrace the healing power of admission and the radiant effect it can have on those around us.

In the spring of 2010, I was awarded an honorary degree at the University of Iowa, an institution that was the backdrop for my own painful experience with failure a half century earlier.

I've commented in other places about arriving at Iowa in the fall of 1958 with a whiz-kid reputation and the hopes of my hardworking parents tucked into a new Samsonite suitcase, a high school graduation gift to take me into the wider world.

It was the beginning of a two-year spiral down into a sybaritic maze of too much alcohol, late nights, too many girls, too few classes, parties first and responsibilities last.

As I told the class of 2010 at Iowa, "Woody Allen says ninety percent of life is showing up; I was in the other ten percent."

I also told the Iowa graduates that my freshman year and the year that followed is a metaphorical ankle bracelet I've worn every year since—that my early failure was a kind of house arrest, a reminder of how quickly and how deeply you can sink if you fail to honestly face up to mistakes and act on them swiftly.

These are lessons to be constantly renewed for governments, institutions, faiths, and common interest groups.

THE PAST

Robert McNamara waited more than a quarter century before he acknowledged his mistakes in the prosecution of the Vietnam War, first in a book and then in Errol Morris's brilliant documentary, **Fog of War**. An aged McNamara answered Morris's off-screen questions and tried to explain the fog of war, the timeworn expression that should—but too seldom does not—remind us that war is not a mathematical or chemical exercise with a fixed outcome.

It is a deadly mixture of anger, hubris, passion, culture, justification and vengeance, ignorance and delusion, patriotism and courage. McNamara's recollection of the Cuban missile crisis, when President Kennedy and his civilian advisers chose a diplomatic chessboard move over military options in order to avoid a nuclear showdown, is at once instructive and infuriating.

If McNamara got that, how could he be such an

active agent in prosecuting the Vietnam War and staying silent when his doubts began to harden? In lectures, the Morris documentary, and his own book and writings, McNamara spent his last years trying to explain his actions, but he left behind more questions than answers, more anger than resolution. Nonetheless, he did at least leave cautionary lessons on war and the exercise of power:

"If we can't persuade nations with comparable values of the merit of our cause, we'd better reexamine our reasoning."

"In the case of Vietnam we didn't know them well enough to empathize. And there was a total misunderstanding as a result. We saw Vietnam as an element of the Cold War, not what they saw it as: a civil war."

At the end of his life McNamara went to Vietnam as part of his odyssey of self-examination. The former foreign minister of North Vietnam, McNamara recalled, said to him, "Mr. McNamara, you must never have read a history book. If you had, you'd know we weren't pawns of the Chinese or the Russians. Don't you know we've been fighting the Chinese for a thousand years? We were fighting for our independence and we would fight to the last man."

I knew Robert McNamara slightly during my Washington years, when he had moved on to the

World Bank. By then he was a forlorn figure, sitting with his handsome wife, Margie, at Kennedy Center concerts or standing off to the side at big cocktail receptions.

There was none of the bravura of the days of the New Frontier.

When Margie, a woman widely admired in the capital, died, Robert began a giddy affair with a younger woman, raising other questions about his judgment. He was like a character in an Ibsen play, wandering around history's landscape in search of himself as others looked on in bewilderment or still-seething anger.

The last time I saw him was on a New York to Washington, D.C., shuttle flight. By chance we were going through security simultaneously and I said, "Bob, I thought **Fog of War** was very important, a real contribution." He was wearing a long tan raincoat, and his signature slicked-back hair was down to a few strands. He looked at me briefly, nodded, and murmured a thank-you as he hurried on to the gate, no one else seeming to notice this onetime intellectual prodigy who was president of the Ford Motor Company by the time he was forty-six, a star in JFK's Camelot, and a mastermind of a national tragedy.

However sad and poignant his life had become, history will not forgive him for the terrible mistakes he made, for his failure to speak out publicly when he began to realize the execution and the expectation for the war in Vietnam were colossally wrong.

Will Donald Rumsfeld, a principal architect of the war in Iraq, ever have a Robert McNamara epiphany, when he publicly acknowledges his exaggerated sense of certainty that he knew best how to deal with Iraq and Saddam Hussein?

Credit must go to McNamara for parting words that are a worthy legacy for future decision makers in a world where a mighty military arsenal remains an important instrument for defending our national interests when it is used in concert with diplomatic and cultural offensives.

Otherwise, as we have learned, it is an agent of provocation, capable of hardening anti-American attitudes while attempting to defeat or diminish real and perceived threats to our national security. No one understands that better than modern military commanders, most of whom these days have advanced degrees in political science or history or have spent a year as White House fellows or as fellows at the Council on Foreign Relations.

They're the front line in the fog of war and pay the heaviest price in the burden of responsibility for loss of life or debilitating wounds among their troops. They take the blame for policy failures that should be traced to civilian armchair generals, militant think tank theorists, and sunshine patriots.

In Iraq and Afghanistan, America's longest wars ever, our best and brightest Army generals were tasked with what proved to be a mission almost impossible: eliminate a terrorist sanctuary, create democratic rule, engender pluralism and a flourishing economy, and provide internal security in two Islamic nations where tribal authority and division is an essential part of the national DNA.

To be sure, some of the military commanders in the combat theaters believed too deeply in their "can-do" training, seeing progress where it was temporary at best. To my eye, very often their perceptions were distorted by the lens of Western conditioning trained on Middle Eastern realities. In the West, we're accustomed to a beginning, middle, and end of conversations, problems, and disputes. In the Middle East, there is a beginning, maybe a middle, and rarely an end.

The best of the commanders understood that, one telling me as late as 2010, "We're just now beginning to understand the Afghan culture." Consequently, the roll call of generals who were retired without glory because they failed to complete that improbable mission is a little-remarked-upon consequence of our involvement. John Abizaid, Rick Sanchez, Dave McKernan, Stanley McChrystal: All are three- or four-star generals whose careers collided with the flawed strategies of their civilian bosses.

Before he initiated his successful surge against continuing terror in Iraq, General David Petraeus spent a year at Fort Leavenworth, Kansas, studying the problem of how to reverse the steady erosion of American power in Iraq and use the anger of Shiite chiefs against Sunni fighters.

Astonishingly, he was not given that assignment until we were four years into the war.

John Abizaid, a longtime student of the Middle East and fluent in Arabic, is known to be frustrated by the absence of a new, overarching U.S. strategy for the region. He has personal as well as professional reasons for his unhappiness. His son, an Army major, has been fighting there for ten years, and he's been wounded twice. A decade later, Abizaid believes, we have more enemies in the region than friends.

The absence of a national discussion of the policies, execution, consequences, and future of the wars in Iraq and Afghanistan in the midterm elections of 2010 was unsettling. In campaigns for seats in the Senate and the U.S. House of Representatives, next to nothing was said about the wars that by that time had killed almost five thousand Americans, wounded more than thirty thousand others, and cost more than a trillion dollars.

The wars in Iraq and Afghanistan define the image of the United States in the Middle East and the subcontinent of Asia and will continue to do so for generations to come. They deserved a prominent place in the passionate debates about the economy, taxes, public debt, and the role of the federal government in our lives.

Yet national security as an issue finished well behind heated arguments about same-sex marriage, the legalization of marijuana, and the real and overblown indiscretions of some candidates. That was a shameful commentary on the substance and nature of modern politics and campaigns.

THE PROMISE

We have another opportunity to raise the level of public discourse: The 2012 presidential election season promises to be one of the most spirited ideological clashes of the last fifty years, powered by the Tea Party's tightly focused message of a greatly reduced federal government influence twinned with the hunger of traditional Republicans to recapture the White House. In defending his four-year stewardship, the president will have the considerable power of the White House bully pulpit to make his case for finishing an incomplete agenda without abandoning federalism as indispensible to the challenge. Citizens demanding a meaningful debate, or even a third party, could have a welcome role, especially if they speak up for a complete airing of military and diplomatic plans.

CHAPTER 17

The Grandparent Lode

FACT: According to a study by Grandparents. com, by 2015, 59 percent of grandparents will be baby boomers, and they're already changing the model of grandparenthood.

As history's most prosperous generation they're inclined to indulge their grandchildren, spending $52 billion a year on goods and services for grandkids. They have also established a new naming pattern for their role.

Contemporary grandchildren no longer see Grandma as the Betty Crocker type in the kitchen. Harvard, MIT, and Brown have grandmother-eligible women as presidents. We're on our third female secretary of state. There are now three women on the U.S. Supreme Court.

The most influential European leader during the economic downturn was Angela Merkel, chancellor of Germany. Brazil has elected its first woman as president, Dilma Rousseff.

In my family, we are dominated by the female sex. I have three daughters and four granddaughters. Male dominance, once taken for granted, is now in play and I fully expect that the twenty-first century will be the first in which women approach full parity.

QUESTION: How do contemporary grandparents fit into this new reality and keep pace with the evolution of opportunity and expectation? Should there be a new model of grandparenting?

THE PAST

As I think back on my parents and grandparents, somehow they were always more mature than their ages and always active citizens. Or perhaps it was just expected of them, a condition of their time in the Great Depression and World War II. They went from their teenage wardrobes to suits and ties, sensible shoes, and grown-up dresses. Those who didn't conform were likely to be thought of as not entirely trustworthy, inspiring comments such as "Oh, you know, Bill just doesn't want to grow up."

Until John F. Kennedy came along, men in their twenties wore hats better suited to men in their forties. Jackie Kennedy, just thirty-one when her husband was elected, was a welcome change for young women who had come of age with their mothers looking more like Mamie Eisenhower than any of the Kennedy women.

It went well beyond wardrobes. The Organization Man was expected to get in line and wait his turn. Women were expected to marry early, have babies early, and go gray in their late forties. Early marriage was part of the compact of a purposeful life.

THE PRESENT

Fast-forward to the generational conceit of my age group: We think we'll be forever young, with the latest running shoes, faded denims, leather jackets, and more toys than our kids.

We can spend now and catch up later, for as Fats Domino sang, "Let the Good Times Roll."

Together Meredith and I intellectually understood that when our daughters married they'd have children and we'd become grandparents, but I don't think we saw ourselves as "Grandma and Grandpa," an old, white-haired couple in tweeds wearing only sensible shoes.

Me with grandparents Ethel and Jim Conley,
Aunt Marcia, and my mother,
Jean Brokaw, in 1941

When we became grandparents we were determined, I think, to carry that attitude forward, to give that role fresh meaning, however surprised we may have been by the fact of grandparenthood itself. We felt we were still young and on the come line of life, and that would connect us to our grandchildren in a new manner.

First, there was the naming thing. What would be we called? Meredith immediately said she wanted to be called Nan, the endearing name of her beloved maternal grandmother. I didn't have a family reference. My grandparents were, in fact, Grandma and Grandpa.

I remember the reaction of Robert Redford when he became a grandfather to two energetic munchkins. We were walking out of a restaurant after a day of skiing. Bob was every inch the Sundance Kid, lean and athletic in boots, blue jeans, and a buckskin jacket. Bystanders gave him the long, admiring stares reserved only for the biggest stars.

Suddenly his red-haired toddler grandkids came running after him, calling out, "Grandpa Bob, Grandpa Bob!" Bob turned and scooped them up, laughing, realizing he'd been busted. Loud enough for his fans to hear, he said, "Not in public, kids. Not in public."

Informally I surveyed friends and others who were also entering this new, welcome, and yet unaccustomed place in life. A dashing airline pilot I met at a Jackson Hole cocktail party said with a self-aggrandizing air, "I've told my grandson to call me Sport."

I preferred the mischievous response of my friend Peter Osnos, the book publisher. "I have them call me Elvis," he said. "What do they know?"

A longtime friend in South Dakota, Larry Piersol, a federal judge, was plainly pleased when his grandchild spotted him wearing a large hat at the family farm and immediately began calling him Cowboy. A New York neighbor, a distinguished psychiatrist, is a Belgian native, so he came up with Le Grand Papa.

Another new grandfather about my age had recently married a younger woman and insisted that his grandson call him by his first name, Ben. And so he did, and the two of them became very close. When Ben visited his grandson's preschool on grandparents' day the child looked up and said, "Ben! What are you doing here?" Ben replied, "It's grandparents' day. I'm your grandfather." The child's eyes widened and he said, "You **are**?"

THE PROMISE

Some of what I've already discovered is that my generation has to race to keep up with the world of our grandchildren. By the time they're six or seven, they're into the dazzling world of information technology, sitting at computer terminals with their own log-ins and favorite sites, playing video games that are much more engaging than the Dick and Jane books of our youth.

The small screen, I've discovered, can be a mutually rewarding meeting place for grandparents and their grandchildren. Email, Skype, and Facebook are happy new forms of communication across generational lines. The latest arresting image on YouTube or a virtual tour of a location in the news may not completely replace "Over the river and through the woods to grandmother's house we go," but they can be an agreeable conduit between generations widely separated by age. That electronic connection is still very much a work in progress, but it has infinite possibilities.

This new generation is also growing up on a palette in which the colors are much more vivid than they were for most of us my age. Their world reflects the steady rise in ethnic integration, from classrooms to after-school activities, television shows and commercials, movies and public life. Well before Barack Obama became the first African American president, there were black, Latino, and Asian school administrators, mayors, and members of Congress and city councils.

When NBC broadcast a retrospective of my

journalism career it included coverage of the civil rights movement out of Atlanta in the sixties. Our San Francisco granddaughters, Claire and Meredith, at the time eight and six years old, were stunned and upset by the images of black people being sprayed with fire hoses and beaten as they marched for their rights. "What was that all about?" they demanded to know of their mother. It was entirely alien to their experience.

They had a similar reaction when in the winter of 2010 I did a lengthy report during the Vancouver Olympics on Gander, Newfoundland, which became a safe port in the storm of uncertainty during the 9/11 attacks. Thirty-seven transatlantic flights and their seven thousand passengers headed to the United States were ordered to land at Gander as part of the airspace shutdown.

The generous and matter-of-fact manner in which the Gander community took in all those strangers on such short notice—fed them, comforted them, and provided beds and even clothing, all at no cost—was so inspiring I suggested to my son-in-law Allen and daughter Jennifer that they watch with Claire and Meredith, by then thirteen and eleven years old.

It didn't occur to me or to their parents that the 9/11 attacks, which are so vivid for us, occurred when they were just four and two. As a result they had no clear memory of that awful time and so they rushed to Google to learn more.

For my part, I realized that America has been at war in Afghanistan and Iraq during most of their lives, but because they have no family members or friends involved, that, too, is not part of their active consciousness. The tedious security procedures at airports are for them routine; they've never known any other way to board a plane.

Like every generation, their time is being defined by new realities, many of them unforeseen but with certain advantages. When each of our grandchildren was born I had the same thought: Welcome. You're off to a good start. You've been born in America into loving, stable families with strong traditions of parenting.

I was never more proud of our middle daughter, Andrea, an executive at Warner Music, than when she was frazzled one Sunday morning while dealing with thirty-month-old Vivian and twelve-month-old Charlotte, trying to give each newly awakened toddler breakfast and attention.

I said, "Motherhood is a lot more demanding than you expected, right?" Andrea paused in the middle of putting a fresh diaper on Charlotte, laughed, and said, "Yeah, Dad, but it is so much **fun.**" She wasn't kidding, this free-spirited Berkeley graduate who spent her twenties and most of her thirties hanging out at rock clubs and concerts, trying to find the next Bruce Springsteen.

Jennifer, our eldest daughter and a physician, shares the joy of parenting with her sister as she shepherds her two daughters through preteen and teenage commitments to school, chorus, soccer, field trips to local attractions, and summer trips to Italy and London.

Jennifer has started a new business as a consulting physician after twelve hard years working in San Francisco and Albuquerque emergency rooms, but she's determined not to dial back her attention to Claire and Meredith or her husband, Allen, a prominent and very busy radiologist.

She recognizes the pressures for women of her generation who want to do it all, including, in her case, a demanding training regimen for long-distance swimming in San Francisco Bay.

"Dad," she'll say, "it wears me out but I know it's worthwhile."

Sarah, our youngest, is not married at age forty-one and with every passing year the idea of becoming a single mother plays a larger role in her life. Frozen embryos, a surrogate, and adoption are subjects a new generation of grandparents have come to know in a way our parents could not have imagined. A clinical therapist, Sarah transformed her personal and professional experience with these issues and others affecting modern young women into a popular book called **Fortytude: Making the Next Decades the Best Years of Your Life— Through the 40s, 50s, and Beyond.**

Exploring the myriad questions facing women in their forties is another manifestation of the social and cultural evolution of Sarah's generation. Confronting these changes as a grandparent is a handy way of calibrating the course of our life histories. When I participated in a grandparents' day at Claire and Meredith's school in the fall of 2009, a teacher asked the grandparents and her students to record side-by-side accounts of life in the seventh grade for the two generations. All the grandparents except one who had attended a public school in the Bronx remarked on the de facto and legal separations of the races in their seventh-grade experiences. We also commented on the inequality of opportunities between boys and girls, especially in athletics.

The grandchildren seemed amused and slightly bewildered by what I am sure they considered to be ancient history. Their lists made no reference to race or gender. They began with computers and video games. They also call their teachers by their first names—remember, this was in San Francisco—a practice that in my time would have meant a note to the principal's office about the troublemaker in the back row.

It was a smart and provocative exercise for the kids and their grandparents alike, one I filed away as a future conversation starter when entertaining my grandchildren.

Here are some differences we didn't get into: When Meredith and I married young—she was twenty-one and I was twenty-two—we had just graduated from college, and everything we owned, mostly wedding presents, fit in the backseat of a Chevy II, one of the first compact cars. We struck out for Omaha and never looked back or called home for money or help.

Now fully half of young Americans between the ages of eighteen and twenty-four still live at home, most of them without a job. That's an increase of 37 percent since 1970. In a book entitled **Not Quite Adults: Why 20-Somethings Are Choosing a Slower Path to Adulthood, and Why It's Good for Everyone,** authors Richard Settersten and Barbara E. Ray remind us that baby boomers, who were so quick to leave their own parents, often enjoy having their children around a while longer, providing financial assistance and advice. Moreover, Settersten and Ray discovered that many young adults are leery of rushing to sign on with an employer who feels no loyalty to them.

They quote a young Nevada woman working her way through college who said, "I think our generation knows that we cannot rely on the government or a company in the future so we have to take care of business ourselves; do these qualities breed loyalty? NO. It simply causes people to base their lives on something of more permanence, such as friends and family."

To that I would add, "including grandparents." It is a new relationship we're all working our way through. If there are rules for connectivity between grandparents and their grandchildren, I seem to have been otherwise engaged the day they were handed out. The best summary is now a well-worn comment: "If I had known how much fun grandchildren would be I would have had them first."

I do have a few learned-on-the-job observations. The truest seems to be this one:

When raising your own children, bribery was a form of white-collar crime. For a grandparent, bribery is a business plan.

It is part of the unspoken Grandparent Code of Behavior that it is okay to buy grandchildren all the ice cream they want, their first bicycles, or even pay for their education. The most ordinary gestures can pay off. During a vacation I made a point of bringing my youngest grandchildren hot oatmeal every morning. Within a day I was greeted with squeals of laughter as they shouted out, "Oatmeal man, here's the oatmeal man." It brought back memories of my own grandfather, a man of extremely meager financial means. When he'd babysit the three Brokaw boys there was no thought of going to the local diner or bowling alley café.

He had a limited capacity in the kitchen, so for breakfast, lunch, and dinner he'd fix us the one dish he had mastered: pancakes. During one three-day stay we must have consumed close to five dozen pancakes.

Grandma Ethel was appalled when she returned, but we assured her we had loved every morsel.

It is also important for our generation of grandparents to go beyond the material and share with our grandchildren our cultural, political, and personal values, to help prepare them for the vastly different circumstances of their future.

When I shared these thoughts with our eldest daughter, Jennifer, she immediately said, "I don't want some sappy letter to my kids talking about the good old days in a Hallmark card kind of way." I promised her I would try to avoid tales of walking to school through Great Plains blizzards or working in a rock quarry for a dollar an hour, even though those were instructive and formative experiences.

As my generation and the baby boomers have

learned, we seem to have a much closer relationship with our grandchildren, just as we do with our children, than our grandparents and parents did with us. We're learning the seemingly infinite uses of the new information technology together. We share common tastes in wardrobes and lifestyles. The chances that my parents would wear blue jeans and running shoes, and go biking or cross-country skiing on weekends, were about as great as Billy Graham opening an ashram.

My generation and the boomers have grown up believing the world needs to hear from us. We've had an ongoing dialogue with our children, so why not just extend that to the grandchildren?

I live in a world that my grandchildren will occupy, as my grandparents did not. They were confined geographically and culturally to the rural Midwest even though they had met in Minneapolis. Their lives were spent first on a farm and then in a succession of small towns as my grandfather found work where he could.

They lived out their senior years in a tiny tidy mobile home, not nearly as spacious as even the most modest SUV I see these days plying the interstate highways of the American West. In the summer months I'd stop by and we'd squeeze together in what passed for the living room and watch the Major League Baseball game of the week on their twelve-inch black-and-white television.

Grandpa wore his Irish sentimental side like a comfortable cardigan, tearing up and sniffling whenever the national anthem was played on television before the game began. Grandma Ethel was a Baker, a no-nonsense WASP who would hiss, "Jim, for God's sake, stop. It's a baseball game, not a memorial service."

Thanks to the television they had an electronic window on a world they never expected to see and certainly didn't expect to experience. Their lives were defined by that small trailer and wherever my parents would take them once they could no longer afford a car, but I remember no complaints. They were cheerful and interested in the news of the day. Ethel even sat by my side when as a family we watched Elvis's first appearance on **The Ed Sullivan Show**.

Mother and Dad failed to see his appeal, but when it was over Grandma said, "He seems like a nice young man; I hope he makes a lot of money."

Fast-forward to my life and relationship with my grandchildren and it is a universe of shared experiences, from urban life to travel, culture, and current events. We have much more of a shared prism through which we see life.

Five-year-old Vivian is a dim sum aficionado. Once Claire and Meredith were with me on a beach when a waitress approached. I was wondering what to order the girls when Claire said in a clear, confident voice, "We'd like two virgin piña coladas. Tom, will you join us?"

For all their worldliness, I hope they also have an appreciation of what went before, beginning with their families on four sides. After all, they are an extension not just of gene pools but also of experiences, dreams, and lessons.

CHAPTER 18

September of My Years

A few years ago I was invited to be a guest on the Sirius XM satellite radio show **Siriusly Sinatra,** devoted to the life and artistry of the man known as the Voice, Ol' Blue Eyes, the Chairman of the Board—Frank Sinatra, probably the greatest American entertainer of my lifetime.

I'd long been a fan of his music and a student of his larger-than-life place in American culture that stretched from show business to politics to the shadowy world of the mob and beyond. That night it was mostly about his music, and I selected as one of my favorite Sinatra recordings "It Was a Very Good Year," the love song to life.

The show in which I participated is repeated from time to time, and when I turned seventy a friend of the same age called to say he'd been listening to it while driving on a dark road on a stormy night in Wyoming. He found the selection of "It Was a Very Good Year" at once evocative and unsettling—unsettling because of that haunting last verse.

It is preceded by paeans to small-town girls and soft summer nights, when I was seventeen; girls who lived up the stair with perfumed hair that came undone when I was twenty-one; blue-blooded girls of independent means with chauffeured limousines when I was thirty-five.

Then, this:

> But now the days grow short;
> I'm in the autumn of the year
> And now I think of my life as vintage wine,
> From fine old kegs,
> From the brim to the dregs,
> And it poured sweet and clear.
> It was a very good year.

That's it. From small-town girls and soft summer nights to a life as wine from the brim to the dregs.

For so long the autumn of my years seemed to be a distant season. But now, inexorably, that season is upon me. While like everyone I'd like to put time back on the clock of my life, I have no rational reason to wish for a reset.

Rather, my short and long objectives are to make the most of the time remaining and to get through the autumn with grace, compassion, and always a commitment to leaving the world a little better place for family and everyone.

As my professional obligations contract, I have no illusion about the need for one more gray head saying, "Now in my day . . ." My familial role has taken on a new form, one that Meredith and I relish.

THE PRESENT

In the sunset years of life and marriage, we find we need to blend each other's strengths and judgment as we deal with a more complicated world, the role of grandparenting, and the financial, emotional, and physical management of the years we have left. Gratefully and in unspoken ways we came to that conclusion simultaneously, and we're working through it in tandem.

How we manage these years, I suspect, will not go unnoticed by our children and grandchildren, just as Meredith and I watched our parents and grandparents as they began what has come to be known as their senior years.

Earlier I noted that today the experiential gap between generations is narrower than it was then. Grandparents and grandchildren share the same tastes in wardrobe, music, movies, technology, and culture to a far greater degree than they once did. (I do wonder how children forty years from now will react to the profusion of tattoos among their grandparents, who are now in their twenties. Or body piercing. "Grandma, where else on his body does Grandpa have a tat of a snake?")

This common turf means grandparents have a unique and welcome role in helping parents set a course for youngsters through the meteor shower of choices the information age brings. What is wise use and what is distraction for the sake of distraction? What is unacceptable, by any standard?

My generation has a unique opportunity to learn something new and perform an important public service simultaneously. Grandparents my age were witness to the cruelties of racial segregation and the violence that erupted when it was challenged. How many people my age and slightly younger had their first lessons in shocking injustice as they watched the fire hoses and dogs turned on the peaceful demonstrators in Birmingham and Selma, or the epithets and twisted expressions of hate that greeted the well-dressed black students walking up the steps of Little Rock Central High School?

Now there's a new form of injustice in schools across the nation: the anonymous taunts and vitriolic mocking designed to hurt and belittle a target for his or her adolescent awkwardness, sexual orientation, or ethnicity.

There have been bullies as long as there has been adolescence, but the Internet tools of videos, anonymous postings, and profane attacks have taken this ancient cruelty to a new level. It is an appropriate subject for parents, schools, communities, and grandparents to take up with the youngsters on the giving and receiving end.

Race is a subject that can open the door to that discussion.

Socially, contemporary grandparents often comment on the color blindness of their grandchildren. However racially tolerant members of my generation may have been, most of them attended segregated schools and lived in racially segregated societies north and south, east and west. Two generations later, their grandchildren live in a time when race is steadily moving away from segregation and toward assimilation.

But bullying is, alas, an exception to the growing place of racial tolerance, and it is in that arena that grandparents can and should be proactive mentors within their families and in schools as volunteers. My generation can bear witness to the shameful treatment of people of color and the hope that almost all of us had that we could move beyond it.

That we have made great progress is testimony first to the courage and vision of the people of the movement, led by Dr. Martin Luther King, Jr., but also to the determination of the rest of the population to march beyond the stain of institutionalized and de facto racism. It should be a matter of generational pride, just as the acknowledgment and diminution of bullying can be a matter of pride for our grandchildren.

To do that we have to find the cyber fusion between our grandchildren and our use of this technology. Websites could be established for interactive conversations and re-publication of the most disturbing images from the civil rights struggle. Online word games could be lessons in hurtful, even hateful, language. It could be an exercise that would help heal the wounds within our generation while providing a forum for intergenerational understanding.

The discussions need not be confined to bigotry or social cruelty. What about a dialogue on the public use of language? When did the F-word become acceptable outside the locker room or barroom? Tell me about your purple hair. Is it only me or do others wonder what the grandparents of the randy, exhibitionist cast of **Jersey Shore** think when they watch Snooki and Paulie and their antics? For that matter, how would you like Paris Hilton as a granddaughter or Charlie Sheen as a grandson? Curious minds want to know.

Attention to personal health and extended longevity are also benchmarks for our generation worth celebrating for the benefit of our grandchildren. At a reunion of high school friends recently—all of us seventy years old or older—I asked, "Who in our town was seventy when we were in high school?" I stumped the gathering. Finally one of the old gang remembered a banker who may have lived his three score and ten. Men, especially, were dying in our town in their late fifties and early sixties with distressing regularity.

In their case, lifestyle was a major factor. They grew up in a world of cigarettes and cigars, marbled beef, mashed potatoes and gravy, fried chicken and butter on everything (even on a slice of cake for my dad), all-you-can-eat buffets, and whipped cream lathered on whatever was for dessert. God forbid they would be caught jogging or biking. Walking from the golf cart to the bar at the end of a motorized round of eighteen holes was about the extent of their regular exercise.

My father and both of Meredith's parents died before they were seventy. My mother lives on into her nineties, thanks, in part, I believe, to a move to California where her lifestyle took on a healthier mien.

Meredith and I have been physically fit since our twenties when we both gave up smoking and began a regular exercise regimen, so our grandchildren have no reason to focus on our diet. I suspect, however, that they may be aware of our appetite for "things." As a result, and for our own ease of mind as well as setting the right kind of grandparent example, we're shrinking, not expanding, our material world.

Our generation has not been a model of temperate materialism, even as we embraced and initiated what has come to be known as the environmental movement. "Reduce, reuse, and recycle" should become our mantra when organizing the next stage of our lives, as an example to the generations that follow.

The psychic and physical energy required to manage too many toys can drain the pleasure of having them.

There is a form of schizophrenia that comes with having grown up with the sensibilities of Great Depression–era parents and the acquisitive traits of my generation. I sometimes open a cabinet filled with seldom-used dishes or sweaters or whatever and feel a wave of guilt, thinking, "We must eat dinner off those plates tonight and I'll wear two of the sweaters!"

"Need" should overwhelm "want" in these years, and our needs should grow smaller and smaller as we advance in age. For too many baby boomers, however, need has taken on a new meaning in the Great Recession, which came along at exactly the wrong time in their lives. As a group, boomers have been on a long joyride of "spend for today and worry about tomorrow two days from tomorrow." It was not only the largest generation in American history but also the wealthiest and most determined to spend, spend, spend.

When the economy took a steep dive, so did the assumptions of baby boomers, now grandparents. Their home values plummeted, their retirement accounts dried up or were greatly reduced, and their expectations for the future took a dark turn. Even financially secure boomers were unsettled by the speed and the reach of the downturn.

It has been, at best, a sobering experience and I do not mean to diminish its effects, but it can also be an instructive lesson to future generations. With our help, grandchildren can learn from our experience. At their age, net worth has little real meaning. It is our love and life they want to share—but we can impart the lessons of managing for the future and not just for instant gratification.

For those of us who were lucky enough to catch the wave of financial security, we can give up a lot and continue to live at a standard unimaginable when we were starting out. It is a matter of reordering priorities.

For me, I was helped, as always, by my mother,

Grandma Jean, a child of the early twentieth century, a survivor of hard times, and a living exemplar of everyday wisdom.

When she was ninety-three years old Mother spent a few days in Montana at a family reunion at our remote ranch. It wasn't an easy trip. She has limited mobility because of arthritis in her spine, so we borrowed a wheelchair and made some modifications in her bedroom of our hundred-year-old farmhouse.

It's a small house by modern standards, just two bedrooms—one up and one down—but a wrap-around addition on the river side added a dining room, fireplace, and sitting area. The kitchen is functional but not a candidate for a Martha Stewart taping.

Altogether I doubt the original house plus the addition add up to 1,100 square feet, including the porch and what we in the West call the mudroom, a back entry where muddy boots and wet jackets are shed.

Mother appeared every morning at the kitchen table, dressed in a light robe, complaining mildly about the cool Montana dawns and sometimes asking, "Where am I?" To help her through her confusion I would quickly ask questions about her childhood on the South Dakota farm where she started life.

THE PAST

She'd pause over her scrambled eggs, look to the distance, and say, "My father made me eat oatmeal every morning in front of the big black kitchen stove where my mother made toast. I hated the oatmeal—still do—but we made wonderful ice cream."

And she'd be off, recalling horse-and-buggy trips to town to buy blocks of ice and the hurried trips back to the farm to store the ice in an insulated icebox that had no electrical refrigeration.

"It was a lot of work," she'd say. "We'd have to chip away at the ice with a pick and hand-crank the real cream and sugar we used, but it was so good." Her expression would become puzzled and she'd say aloud, to no one in particular, "What were the names of our horses? I used to remember them all. I think Gladys was the horse that drank from the stock tank and then leaked all the water out of her mouth all the way back up the hill."

Her gaze would drift to our modest kitchen and she'd say, "Our house then was about the size of this room and maybe one other," then she'd return to her breakfast, shaking her head slightly.

I'd sit and watch, occasionally prompting her with questions but mostly trying to see in my mind's eye a slide show of her life.

With my father, she got through the Depression and World War II by getting up every morning with the same set of values as the day before: family first, hard work, faith, thrift, moderation, and community.

Mother, particularly, was interested in politics, an admirer first of FDR and then Harry Truman, who physically resembled her father. Mother and Dad were registered Democrats but skeptical about John F. Kennedy's stylish ways; Hubert Humphrey was more their kind of guy, a native of South Dakota who took Main Street with him wherever he went.

The fifties were boom years for my parents and other working-class folks. They bought their first home and first new car. My father was making respectable wages as a hard-hat-wearing, lunch-box-carrying foreman for the U.S. Army Corps of Engineers on the big flood control and hydroelectric dams being constructed on the Missouri River.

They were saving money for my college education and spending Saturday nights having dinner, drinking a few highballs, and dancing with friends at the local Elks Club. Life was good.

Like so many members of their generation, they were unprepared for the upheaval of the sixties. They were opposed to the war in Vietnam but even more opposed to the idea of college deferments from the draft. When my brother shipped out as a marine, headed for Vietnam (he made it back), my father called me to rail against college boys getting a pass.

I initially made a feeble defense but quickly conceded he was right. We had equally spirited arguments about hair length and militant movements.

The night Mike left for the war, Mother and Dad were on a road trip back to South Dakota from visiting us in Atlanta. They stopped in Tennessee and, anxious about their youngest son's safety, they uncharacteristically hit the hotel bar for a couple of belts.

Mother had her first taste of Jack Daniel's, Tennessee's homegrown sour mash whiskey.

Years later she would remember that stressful night and say, "But I was helped by that good whiskey—what do they call it? Tennessee walking horse whiskey?" The Brokaw boys would tease her about her drinking naïveté. She never did become a Jack and Coke kind of mom.

When my father retired in the early eighties he and Mother moved into a two-bedroom condominium surrounded by the lush vegetation of Southern California in a large Orange County retirement community. They'd return to South Dakota for the summer months, but it was clear California was becoming a large part of their lives.

Dad would spend his weekdays as if still on the job, in the community woodworking shop, making traditional baby cradles for younger friends who were giving him a growing brood of surrogate grandchildren to go with his own. Winter evenings he'd often step out onto his balcony overlooking the flowering trees and sun-washed bougainvillea bushes, laugh, and say aloud, "If the boys in Bristol could see me now," a reference to his hardscrabble hometown on the northern prairie of South Dakota.

In 1983, his journey from a childhood of deprivation and despair to working-class prosperity, respectability, and real, measureable accomplishment came to an abrupt end. He died of a massive coronary at the age of sixty-nine the week before I was to begin anchoring the **NBC Nightly News**.

Mother wisely concluded, "South Dakota doesn't need another widow." She moved permanently to California and for the next thirty years she had a life she never could have imagined as a young woman.

She returned to Europe for a second time, cruised through the Panama Canal, and found a male friend in her bridge club. Together they sailed the Alaska coastline. She went to concerts in Los

Angeles and became an enthusiastic fan of the Angels of the American League and the Lakers of the NBA.

When I got her an autographed picture from Kobe Bryant she was thrilled, until he got in trouble in Colorado. Then she took down the picture but did not throw it away. When the Lakers began to win championships again, she put Kobe back on the wall and never conceded that she might have been guilty of a sliding scale of worthiness.

When age and infirmities began to overrun her enthusiasm for an active life she retreated to her assisted living apartment without rancor or complaint. She would occasionally say, matter-of-factly, "I've lived long enough" or "I never expected to live this long." Yet she would soldier on, and made a difficult trip to Montana for a gathering of her boys and our families.

She'd sit in her wheelchair at lunch in our rustic lodge, gazing out at the river running through the property, the thick, golden grass on the hillsides, the stately cottonwoods, Douglas firs, and aspen trees framing the distant mountains, and ask, "Now where are we?" When I answered, "We're on our ranch, Mom. Remember, Meredith and I bought this twenty years ago. You've been here before."

She'd shake her head slightly, pat me on the hand, and then, noticing I was wearing my fishing cap

In her nineties, Grandma Jean remains
the family role model.

indoors, she'd silently gesture with her arthritic hands for me to take it off.

No caps at lunch in her presence, ever.

When she returned to California, Meredith and I reflected on the lessons of our grandparents and how they have stayed with us.

Meredith's paternal grandfather, a no-nonsense but lovable country physician, was known to everyone as simply "Doc." He taught her to drive on isolated rural roads when she could barely see over the steering wheel and played daily word games when she visited him and her grandmother Bird during the summer.

Doc was an amateur geneticist and such a wise observer of the political world that George McGovern, South Dakota's liberal senator, always made it a point to stop for a visit when he was in the vicinity, even though Doc was a card-carrying Republican.

Doc's been gone for more than half of Meredith's life and yet she remembers his many influences on her as if they were passed along yesterday. Her maternal grandparents, Gramp and Nan, were equally important to her formative years, in part because they shared Doc and Bird's values, if not their politics. Gramp was a populist Democrat when he met Franklin Delano Roosevelt as a vice presidential candidate in the twenties.

They got along well, and FDR appointed Gramp to New Deal–era commissions during the Depression and World War II. When Meredith's father was gone for five long years during the war, she lived with Gramp and Nan in their home next to the Masonic lodge where he was executive secretary, a position that paid little but perfectly positioned him as a wise counselor to what passed for the community's power structure.

It was in their home that Meredith developed a lifelong interest in politics and the news of the day. Meredith, Gramp, and Nan would gather around the large cabinet radio in the living room with Nan's doilies draped over the sofa and Gramp's White Owl cigar burning in the standing ashtray.

Like Doc, his good friend and a favorite political debating opponent, Gramp was revered for his tireless enthusiasm for good works and pride in all things South Dakota. Thanks to his FDR connection, he was a ranking official in the March of Dimes campaign, the crusade to find a cure for polio.

Gramp was literally larger than life, at six feet five and close to three hundred pounds, always with a black Stetson and, until late in his life, a lit cigar in his hand. He liked a shot of whiskey and a beer chaser, the cowboy cocktail known as a "bump and

Guy and Edyth Harvey,
Meredith's maternal grandparents

a beer." His childhood was shaped by the calloused-hands way of life of West River country, the rolling grassland and badlands west of the Missouri River.

Nan, a quiet, diminutive woman, was raised in the same area on a remote, economically marginal ranch. During the deathly flu epidemic of 1918, she rode on horseback from ranch to ranch, doing what she could to help families who were losing members to the lethal strain of influenza.

She would recall with a small smile how she and her sister would help with haying in the summertime. Often when they would buck up a load of fresh-cut hay the air would fill with rattlesnakes that had been caught in the harvest.

Gramp had an extensive vocabulary in Lakota, the language of the state's Sioux tribes, and taught Meredith to count in the Indian way. As a ten-year-old he met Calamity Jane on a Sunday morning in a Fort Pierre bar. He was on his way to Sunday school when he found an empty whiskey bottle, which could be redeemed for a nickel.

"There was this rough-looking woman at the bar on Sunday morning," he liked to recall, and "she made fun of my tie, grabbing it and cutting it off with a big knife. I began to cry and she felt bad so she handed me a silver dollar. That's when I found out it was Calamity Jane."

My favorite Gramp story, however, involved the

Good Friends

The above is a picture of Ye Old Secretary and Dr. Auld at the time of the presentation of the 60-year palm. Ye Old Secretary has not received his palm yet, but has a half-century button. Also we have a lot in common. No, it is not politics — anybody knowing the two gentlemen can easily figure that out — but in common we are both grandfathers of five wonderful children of Dr. and Mrs. Merritt A. Auld, and we have got to add, one great granddaughter. We have been friends for many a year, and as far as the Old Sec goes, we were very happy to be at the presentation.

Meredith's grandfathers, Guy Harvey
and Clarence "Doc" Auld: One was a
Democrat, the other a Republican,
but politics never affected
their deep friendship.

death of his hero, President Roosevelt, in 1945. Think of the timing. The end of World War II is in sight. The promise of prosperity is bright after fifteen years of economic depression and the trauma of war. Suddenly, the great man who led the nation through all of that is gone.

For Gramp, it was also a deeply felt personal loss. "I locked myself in my room for two days," he said, "smoked cigars, drank whiskey, and cried. Finally, I came out"—and here his voice would drop an octave as he said, "and Edith [Nan] understood."

Those stories and the influences of Doc and Bird, Gramp and Nan, have stayed with Meredith for more than sixty years.

There were no trust funds or European junkets, no new cars at graduation or fancy watches. Both sets of grandparents would take the grandkids for a week to a rustic cabin on a Minnesota lake in the summer or on a train ride across Canada. Maybe they'd slip a five-dollar bill in a card on a teenager's birthday, but that would be the limit of material gifts.

In remembering them and my grandparents, Meredith and I both have the same recollections: They were always engaged citizens, attentive to local and national politics and international affairs. When I was too young to fully comprehend what he was trying to teach me, my grandfather would open **Time** magazine to trace the maps of World War II. He also suggested to my mother that she keep the encyclopedia in the bathroom so we could read while in the tub or on the john. She resisted, but somehow we all turned out okay anyway.

I like to think that if Doc, Gramp, and my grandpa were still with us they'd be asking, "Have you thought about learning to read and speak in the Chinese language? Or Arabic?"

Meredith remembered her grandfathers getting together and promising not to argue about politics but failing. "Doc and Gramp always had heated but respectful discussions about politics when they got together and they weren't parroting someone else. They did their homework, and anyone listening would be enlightened. It was just part of my growing up."

THE PROMISE

We were blessed to be surrounded by elders who were always active, involved citizens in small ways and large.

What better legacy for one generation to pass along to another? Meredith and I have tried to keep that perspective in mind. If we can have the same influence on our grandchildren as our grandparents had on us, that will be reward enough.

We learned early as grandparents that close-to-the-ground, very personal excursions can lead to some essential truths. A few years ago, Meredith and I took our San Francisco granddaughters on an overnight camping trip to a backcountry cabin in the Montana mountains. It was not an easy hike, leading through trackless timber and up steep slopes, but despite some small-bore protesting about the bugs and the isolation, the girls made it.

After a cookout we explained to Claire and Meredith, then nine and seven, that they would be sleeping inside the darkened cabin, which had been a cowboy's one-room shelter during roundup time. Meredith assured them, "Tom and I will be right outside."

We slipped into our sleeping bags under the stars and listened to the girls' whispers from inside the tiny cabin. Suddenly, the youngest of the two appeared and said in a commanding voice, "Nan, we need an adult in **here**—NOW."

Don't we all?

Sometimes those reminders of adult roles and responsibilities come in unexpected fashion. In June 2006, I was in Montana on a bluff overlooking a grove of conifers alongside the west Boulder River, which was close to flood stage because of the heavy snowpack runoff.

As I stood there a small herd of elk cows—mothers—emerged from the tree line with their new calves. They paused to look at me and apparently decided that I was far enough away to do no harm, and so they stepped into the raging river to lead their children to the grassy pastures on the other side.

It was not an easy crossing. The calves struggled against the current and then had to thrash their way through thick brush on the far bank. One calf failed and was swept downstream, swimming frantically until he reached an eddy and was able to gain a sandbar on the side from which he'd started.

He waded into the river and failed again, repeating the retreat to the eddy and the sandbar. He tried a third time and still didn't make it. When he got back to the sandbar he was trembling, and I wondered, What now?

On the far bank, the rest of the herd waited patiently as the mother of the frightened calf stood at the water's edge and, as God is my witness, nodded her majestic head to him, as if to say, "It's okay; I'm coming to get you."

With that she waded into the river and crossed over to him, nuzzling him for a moment before leading him upstream to an easier passage. They rejoined the rest of the herd and trotted off to greener pastures.

I was so moved by the experience I could barely breathe, and once again I was reminded that every year the creatures of the wild teach me something about life as it should be lived.

I shared the story with our grandchildren and friends over the years, extending the metaphor about maternal care to include the obligation we all have to one another when we reach our own flood-stage rivers. We navigate them successfully when we do it together.

ACKNOWLEDGMENTS

This book first began to take shape in my mind as I traveled across America on U.S. Highway 50 for a study of the American character commissioned by Bonnie Hammer, the enterprising and creative head of USA, the cable channel that is such an important part of the NBC family. Martha Spanninger led our Peacock Productions team on the long road from the eastern shore of Maryland to Sacramento, California, with stops in Washington, D.C.; Ohio; Indiana; St. Louis, Missouri; Kansas; Colorado; and Nevada. In every location I visited with fellow citizens who shared their wisdom, concerns, and determination not to lose the American Dream. I am eternally grateful for their cooperation and insights.

Once the book was under way, I was helped immeasurably by Ruby Shamir, researcher extraordinaire. Her ability to turn out user-friendly and yet sophisticated material on a wide range of inquiries was breathtaking. Ruby, I cannot thank you enough.

As always, Steve Capus, president of NBC News, and my other colleagues were curious, encouraging, and helpful, particularly my indefatigable assistant, Mary Casalino. Sylvie Haller, Clare Duffy, M. L. Flynn, and others involved in the production of NBC News' Education Nation series were especially important in framing the education chapters.

At home, I relied heavily on the cool efficiency of Geri Jansen to keep my personal life on track as I worked my way through this journey. In Montana, I had help from Luke Highley, Catherine McClanahan, Doug Campbell, Max Demars, and others.

This is my sixth book for Random House and none would have happened without the expert guidance, cheering on, and personal loyalty of the great Kate Medina. Kate's unerring compass and friendly persistence kept me on track throughout. No message from her failed to lift my spirits.

Others at Random House without whom I would have faltered include Gina Centrello, Tom Perry, Benjamin Dreyer, Evan Camfield, Paolo Pepe, Carole Lowenstein, Theresa Zoro, Sally Marvin, Barbara Fillon, Karen Fink, Sanyu Dillon, Avideh Bashirrad, Erika Greber, Lindsey Schwoeri, Anna Pitoniak, and Rebecca Pomerantz.

Finally, and especially since this book is a deeply personal statement, I am, more than ever, in awe of the strengths, judgments, and capacity for love of my family. Meredith, my life-mate and irreplaceable lodestar. Jennifer and Allen, Andrea and Charles, Sarah—they all know exactly how to deal with Dad. They're fearless in their advice and unconditional in their love.

Finally, to the grandchildren. Claire, Meredith, Vivian, and Charlotte: This is for you, and I hope it will give you a fraction of the meaning you've added to my life.

PERMISSIONS AND CREDITS

Photographs:
Page xviii: © Audrey Hall
Page 45: © Jimmy Clemons
Page 50: © G.L. Lewis Photography
Page 56: Courtesy of Denise Garison
Page 64: NBC Universal Photo Bank
Page 114: Courtesy of the author
Page 127: NBC Universal Archives
Page 146: NBC Universal Photo Bank
Page 149: Courtesy of Doug Tompkins
Page 153: Courtesy of Make It Right

Page 191: Courtesy of Celia Miner
Page 201: NBC Universal Photo Bank
Page 206: NBC Universal Photo Bank
Page 284: Associated Press
Page 297: Courtesy of the author
Page 326: Courtesy of the author
Page 329: Courtesy of the Brokaw family
Page 331: Courtesy of the Brokaw family

INDEX

ABOUT THE AUTHOR

TOM BROKAW is the author of five bestsellers: **The Greatest Generation, The Greatest Generation Speaks, An Album of Memories, A Long Way from Home,** and **Boom!** A native of South Dakota, he graduated from the University of South Dakota with a degree in political science. He joined NBC News in 1966, serving as the White House correspondent during Watergate and anchoring **Today** on NBC from 1976 to 1981. He was the sole anchor and managing editor of **NBC Nightly News with Tom Brokaw** from 1983 to 2005. He continues to report for NBC News, producing award-winning long-form documentaries and providing expertise during breaking news events. Brokaw has won every major award in broadcast journalism, including two DuPonts, a Peabody, and several Emmys. He is a regular contributor to the op-ed pages of **The New York Times, The Washington Post,** and **The Wall Street Journal,** and to **Time, Newsweek,** and **Men's Journal.** He lives in New York and Montana.

LIKE WHAT YOU'VE READ?

If you enjoyed this large print edition of
THE TIME OF OUR LIVES,
here are two of Tom Brokaw's latest bestsellers
also available in large print.

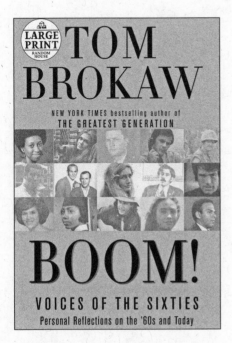

BOOM!
(paperback)
978-0-7393-2682-4
($28.95/$36.95C)

**THE GREATEST
GENERATION**
(paperback)
978-0-375-70569-4
($24.95/$34.95C)

Large print books are available wherever books
are sold and at many local libraries.

All prices are subject to change. Check with your
local retailer for current pricing and availability.
For more information on these and other large print titles,
visit <u>www.randomhouse.com/largeprint</u>.